DAILY DOSE OF
WISDOM

DR. JOSEPH PUTHENPURAKAL

Order this book online at www.trafford.com
or email orders@trafford.com

Most Trafford titles are also available at major online book retailers.

Print information available on the last page.

ISBN: 978-1-4907-9883-7 (sc)
ISBN: 978-1-4907-9884-4 (e)

Trafford rev. 12/20/2019

 www.trafford.com

North America & international
toll-free: 1 888 232 4444 (USA & Canada)
fax: 812 355 4082

DEDICATION

It is said that a man cannot leave a better legacy to the world than a well-educated family. I am glad that I have accomplished that goal. I dedicate this book to my children Jason, MBA, Dr. Tom, Sherin Joseph, MPH, pursuing her MD studies, daughter in law Dr. Kriti, who have made me proud by reaching their educational and career goals by focused and dedicated hard work. I also dedicate this book to my grandsons, Arian, Ishan and future grand children who all, I am sure, will benefit from reading this book as they grow up. I believe that this book "Daily Dose of Wisdom" will serve as a torch of light in their life journey.

"Lives of great men all remind us, we can make our lives sublime, and, departing, leave behind us, footprints on the sands of time" Henry Wadsworth Longfellow. "All our dreams can come true-if we have the courage to pursue them" Walt Disney.

JANUARY 1

"Lives of great men all remind us, we can make our lives sublime, and, departing, leave behind us, footprints on the sands of time".
Henry Wadsworth Longfellow

> *"As for all those who productively lived their lives still have their names carved in the history of times."*

S uccess comes with a keen sense of vision and purpose. No great mind has ever existed without having his vision and purpose of existence lucid to him. All the men of wisdom and glory had secrets of universe unleashed unto them prominent of which were the fleeting nature of the earth and existential potential. It is, thence, they didn't waste their brief stay on earth in chasing the mirage of man-made and worldly pleasures. They had a way of digging down their souls to extract a purpose vague to the ordinary mind and worked towards it. The great men had known how to live while they can and dedicated their fleeting time in serving mankind either directly or indirectly. Which is why their masterly crafts are still engraved in museums and legacy carved in the books. Death couldn't entirely take them away, for their supreme legacy remained. Awareness of the purpose and mindfulness of the future is the key to all successes in life.

JANUARY 2

"If you eat honey, my son, because it is good, if pure honey is sweet to your taste, such, you must know, is wisdom to your soul, if you find it, you will have a future, and your hope will not be cut off"
From Proverbs of Solomon(24-13,14)

> *"What food is to the body; wisdom is to the soul."*

T he world is a delusion for the sensible. He can see through the veils of fallacy and point out the oddity in the system. Wisdom is transcendence from the mundane and ordinary. It comes from a keen sense of understanding of oneself and the surroundings. This sagacity and loftiness in intelligence are achieved after treating ugly flukes as an epiphany descended by God to comprehend the world and its operations. And as hard as it is to attain, so is it to get away with upon possession. Wisdom, when acquired, starts running down the veins, modifies the opinions, reconstructs the intuition and governs one's actions. Upon discovering it, one is introduced to the concealed truths of the world, which, against hope, prepares him for the ugly stroke of luck.

JANUARY 3

"One generation departs and another generation comes, but the world forever stays" The book of Ecclesiastes – chap. 1-4)

"People come and go, but the world remains forever."

This world is a scream into the void which sooner or later diffuses into thin air, just like energy which travels and transforms from one state to another. Such is the nature of the earth as it steals the oxygen of those whose duration is over and generously grants it to those who are just introduced to the world. And in between resides the greed, desire, pleasure, and hunger of a human who is busy chasing after the wind in vain. Human life is but temporary, and the universe only conspires to attain a system of balance in the world. Just as our old cells are worn out and replaced by the new ones to keep our body functioning free of toxins, in the same way, God descends young lives on this globe and takes back those who've had their time and experience. Every minute someone takes his/her last breath leaving behind the others to live on. Whereas, others, over the loss of their loved ones, realize that they all are in-line to depart. In the meantime, the earth keeps on rotating, the world keeps on fostering its planets, and new lives keep going on oblivious of who came before them.

JANUARY 4

"Education is the great engine of personal development. It is through education that the daughter of a peasant can become a doctor, that the son of a mineworker can become the head of the mine, that a child of farm workers can become the president of a great nation. It is what we make out of what we have, not what we are given, that separates one person from another." —Nelson Mandela

> *"Regardless of the conditions, we are born in*
> *and irrespective of the tribulations we bump into,*
> *we're still what we make of ourselves."*

God has sent this spirit of us wrapped in a body habitable to this planet only to invest our expertise in nurturing and protecting the globe that He has splendidly crafted. And humans, the habitants of the world, introduced a standard and disciplined order of doing things which could serve in the best interest of both the residents and the world. So, the education of system and order of the surroundings is as significant as the purpose of one's life. Having a knack for education and passion for knowledge, when Malala wasn't allowed to attend school during the Taliban regime, she didn't surrender to fears and stood up for herself and her school fellows despite the threat to her life. And today she is pursuing a degree in Philosophy, Politics, and Economics at the most renowned University of Oxford, sending the message of courage and resolution across.

JANUARY 5

"How you think is everything: Always be positive. Think success, not failure, beware of negative environment" IBD's 10 Secrets to Success

> *"It all begins and ends with our thinking which is*
> *the primal source of generating action."*

Since ages, experts and philosophers had been crying for us to pick our thoughts wisely because they transform into actions.

The problem begins when our actions determine our habits and breed unhealthy choices. And these unhealthy choices, in turn, become our fate. Hence, the crux is to pick our thoughts correctly, which is the determinant variable of our outlook on life. Positivity yields positive experience and instills gratitude, whereas negativity steers failure and despair. When Steve Jobs was thrown out of his very own creation 'Apple' by the Board of Directors, he didn't stop believing in himself. He gathered a group of intellects from his previous workplace and resolved to take over Apple with his new startup NeXt. A few years later, NeXt bought Apple, and Steve became the CEO again. Had he stopped right there and accepted his failure, things would've been different today. The thoughts of a person have the most significant say in making or breaking him. To all those who have success on their minds, flair in their crafts, and determination in their bones, no power on earth can stop them.

JANUARY 6

"The price of greatness is responsibility" Winston Churchill

"The bigger the person, the more boulders on the shoulders."

Before assigning a big task to a person, God instills in him the courage, determination, and sense of responsibility to carry it out, which is why all the greatest minds that have ever existed had a major role to play for the betterment of society. M.K Gandhi was an ordinary man whose attire would attract criticism from Winston Churchill and got him to receive mistreatment in South Africa. Later, his mission and sense of responsibility got him to become the exceptional leader of India during the wreak havoc of the 20th century.

JANUARY 7

"Always bear in mind that your own resolution to succeed is more important than any other one thing" Abraham Lincoln

"Having success on your mind is the
most significant rule of living."

Faith in self comes from the strength of character. History has it, every inspiring figure of today and yesterday had an element of unwavering faith to them embodied through confidence and relentless devotion toward their passion. Abraham Lincoln lost almost eight elections and two businesses of his life and yet his resolve to succeed got him to reign the USA as the 16th President. Dedication and consistency, even in the face of failure, is the key to achieve all the milestones.

JANUARY 8

"You cannot help men permanently by doing for them what they could and should do for themselves" Abraham Lincoln.

"You cannot change the adverse condition of someone
who isn't adamant on changing his situation."

We, as human beings, feel obliged to attend to the needs of anyone in trouble, pain, or misery. In doing so, we go as far as leading them to the drinking water where only the drinking and swallowing is unto them. At times when we do enough for the people, they ought to lose their sense of esteem, let alone their confidence in themselves, and start relying on us. you ought to know the difference between helping others and making them dependent on you. Feeding the needy is generosity, but spoon-feeding their daily needs is spoiling them and their self-confidence. It is merely and primarily unto a man to decide his fate.

JANUARY 9

"We tend to get what we expect" Norman Vincent Peale

"The human brain is designed to experience what it anticipates."

We tend to play scenarios inside our head – be it overanalyzing our situations or vibes and demeanor of someone else. And what we perceive to be the case eventually becomes one in inside our head. Hence, expectations are either the root of all great occurrences or worst of experiences. And we ought to receive what we anticipate – good or bad. Just like the famous story of elephants who were bound by the ropes since their birth and expected, the ropes would not break even when they were an adult. They expected the life of captivity and that's precisely what they received irrespective of their power and strength against the frail rope which was just one thrust away from freedom.

JANUARY 10

"Become a possibilitarian. No matter how dark things seem to be or actually are, raise your sights and see possibilities-always see them, for they're always there" Norman Vincent Peale

"For everything that exists on this planet, there is a left-wing and a right-wing. For night there is day; for rainfall, there is sunrise; for grief, there is happiness; for weakness there is strength; for wrong there is right, and this is how our life attains balance. Without one wing you cannot enjoy the fruits of the other."

It is during the darkness that one needs to understand and see through the tragedy to get the lesson. And realize during the trial that when winter comes, summer isn't far apart, if agony comes, then joy isn't far apart, and if despair comes, hope is just around the corner. And precisely this is what makes a person rise above the storm. During the Chernobyl disaster, it was Valery Legasov who, despite the mayhem and flared up panic in the city, maintained his nerves and suggested counteractions to mitigate the repeated accidents resulting from the penetration of deadly gases. It is due to his efforts and suggestion of immediate evacuation that saved the lives of the residents of Pripyat.

JANUARY 11

"There is no use whatever trying to help people who do not help themselves. You cannot push anyone up a ladder unless he is willing to climb himself" Andrew Carnegie

> *"God doesn't change the situation of anyone who doesn't have a fair sense of changing it himself."*

You cannot rise a person from the slums of life and then expect from him the mannerism of a literate man if he isn't willing to learn and only up for luxurious bites. You can only push the bicycle of an amateur a few strides, rest of the paddling is for him to do. Junior Johnson, the most prominent athlete of his time, used to smuggle alcohol as a teenager and went to jail because of it. His life transformation began with him getting tired of his own shitty profession and evolved from the brighter side. He employed his motor skills for NASCAR and reportedly won 50 races out of 313. Today, a stretch of highway in his hometown is named after him.

JANUARY 12

"Darkness cannot drive out darkness; only light can do that. Hate cannot drive out hate; only love can do that" Martin Luther King.

> *"It takes water to extinguish the fire, warmth to smother the cold-hearted, love to ward off hate and company to tend to the lonely."*

You cannot fight fire with fire and expect the war to settle without loss of lives. You cannot show wrath against wrath and expect the relationship not to bear the damages after the rage is over. To counter anything of a specific nature, another thing of equal opposite nature is required to neutralize its effects. As a teenager, Kweisi Mfume has had many stints in jail before getting divine guidance and turning his life around by enrolling in a college. Later, his fervent dedication got him elected at the Baltimore City Council, Congress, where he turned up to be the president of NAACP.

JANUARY 13

"Nine-tenths of wisdom consists in being wise in time" Winston Churchill

"Wisdom is in being wise when it's required."

A s we roll on with life, we tend to undergo situations which demand us to act or say the right things just in time so not to miss on the moment or opportunity. A missed opportunity or an unspent moment bring waves of regret later. The reflexes of a human happen to be his biggest weapon. If it couldn't spot the danger approaching, the human is dead – be it while crossing the road, encountering a street criminal or doing any tasks that require vigilance. One's ability to deal with a challenge thrown its' way decides his fate. It is vital for a human to seize the opportunity, live a precious moment, and interpret a situation just in time before it's gone with the wind.

JANUARY 14

"The best thing about the future is that it comes only one day at a time" Abraham Lincoln

"For both, the best and worst days of our lives,
we have one whole day to cater to it."

W e live one day at a time. The tomorrows knock on our doors every morning to remind us of the put aside tasks of yesterday. Each day we take one step towards the future, towards the end.

Therefore, it is required of us to make the most of the day and productively use our time to leave something of value behind. Every person's life is comprised of two days, one which is in favor of him, the other which is against him. The former demands the gratitude from him, whereas the latter demands patience. These two days constitute our life. It was this one succession at a time that made Joseph, a slave in Egypt, the Prime Minister of the country from the life of prison.

JANUARY 15

"My dream is of a place and a time where America will once again be seen as the last best hope of earth" Abraham Lincoln

"Of all the dreams and hopes, my wish to see America becoming the last ray of hope for countries all over the world tops the list".

A braham Lincoln, in his address to US Congress on December 1, hoped for the betterment of America and shared his foresight of watching it become one. Being a wishful, dedicated, and a man of oneiric wisdom, he always imparted the message of hope, justice, and unwavering optimism in the face of adversity. He is a perfect example of a man who relied on his visitation dreams to find solutions to the problems prevailing in his regime. He didn't only pull America from the mayhem of the Civil War but also passed foreign policy in hopes of freeing the slaves and African Americans. Even if his dream didn't warn him about his looming end, his oneiric instinct had always helped him keep his army of generals united and courageous. The day of his assassination, he opened up before his generals and forecasted the legitimate reality to his dream of watching the Union triumphing over the Confederacy and expressed his expectations of America becoming a region of hope for the rest of the world.

JANUARY 16

"We must combine the toughness of the serpent and the softness of the dove, a tough mind and a tender heart" Martin Luther King.

"To be able to balance both, the hard and the soft traits is a skill only the wise can master."

There are two sides to a coin, two hands to clap, two sides to a story, and it even takes two to tango. Human is the most complex of species that God has crafted. He is all about contradictions with a multitude of opposite emotions and powers: happy, sad, good, bad, positive, negative, anger, and joy. Only it is unto human to possess and manage the opposite and contradictory traits in a manner that could develop in him a strength of character. Persephone, the Goddess of Vegetation, was both a beautiful floral maiden and a queen of the underworld and death.

JANUARY 17

"Without courage all other virtues lose their meaning" Winston Churchill

"If virtue is direction, valor is the sacred book."

In everything you do, let courage be the core. The adversities may come and go, but they never leave without teaching you a lesson. To stand with courage in the face of difficulty is the mark of a valorous man.

JANUARY 18

"You're only as good as the people you hire" Ray Kroc

"You are what and whom you recruit."

As a customer, you are mostly what you buy. As an employer, you are precisely what and who you recruit. The skillset of the employee that attracted you while recruiting is the skillset that you deem perfect for the position. Your sense of perfection defines you.

JANUARY 19

"Concentration is my motto – first honesty, then industry, then concentration" Andrew Carnegie

"Build your focus, find an industry, and deliver."

Find a purpose to work on. Once that is done, jot your focus and concentration to work on your desired job. Next is to hunt for a job by looking into job descriptions and specifications. Upon finding one, you are supposed to deliver with all your might.

JANUARY 20

"Surplus wealth is a sacred trust which its possessor is bound to administer in his lifetime for the good of the community" Andrew Carnegie.

"Both wealth and wealthy bear a responsibility toward society."

The purpose of the wealth is to be spent on something that is worth whereas the motive of the wealthy should be to spend it on programs that serves for the betterment of the society.

JANUARY 21

"The best executive is the one who has sense enough to pick good men to do what he wants done, and self-restraint enough to keep from meddling with them while they do it" Theodore Roosevelt

"A good executive knows who to hire, how to get the work done and not be bothersome in the process."

The sign of a good leader is that he knows how to lead his army and what kind of pep-talk is required to drive a certain action. The most important thing that a leader practice is that he doesn't poke his nose in his employees' business after the work is done.

JANUARY 22

"The most valuable of all talents is that of never using two words when one will do" Thomas Jefferson

> *"Of all the talents known to mankind, briefest of speech rules out the rest."*

A short speech is always effective. The longer and more you speak, you tend to miss out the main message. Wise men only speak when they have something important to say. The less you speak, the less are you likely to get in trouble because you never regret the words you don't speak.

JANUARY 23

"We hold these truths to be self-evident: that all me are created equal; that they are endowed by their creator with certain unalienable rights; that among these are life, liberty, and the pursuit of happiness" Thomas Jefferson

> *For the satisfaction of humans, only this idea is enough that we all are alive, liberal, and seeking happiness.*

The mere fact that we are breathing in an independent state, practicing our rites and traditions without objections and setting out to find our purpose of existence are reasons enough for the civilians of a state.

JANUARY 24

"The care of human life and happiness, and not their destruction, is the first and only legitimate object of good government" Thomas Jefferson

An ideal government is the one from the organs
of which its citizens are satisfied.

A good government is the one that takes special care of the needs of its people and attends to their requirements. It sets up institutions to educate the children and encourage business to increase employment opportunities. Whatever it does, it does it for the benefit and betterment of its people.

JANUARY 25

"Eternal vigilance is the price of liberty" Thomas Jefferson

When gets out of hands, liberty invites surveillance.

When the government gives enough liberty to its people, they forget the rulebook and become incapable of differentiating between wrong and right. And that's where the problem begins. It's that's why only optimum liberty should be given for people to stay in their limits.

JANUARY 26

"Choose a job you love and you will never have to work a day in your life" Confucius.

Follow your passion as it never tires you even if you retire.

One must do what he feels like doing. Many men are wasting themselves by employing themselves in the organizations started up by others. It's better to follow your passion and entrepreneur your own startup than to follow the commands of the ones who get their goals achieved through you.

JANUARY 27

"In the middle of difficulty lies opportunity" Albert Einstein

Amidst the storm, you learn to swim.

It is during the hardships that you get to know what strength have you been holding within. It is during the difficulty you are introduced to the new ways of coping with things that are out of your control. All the adversities are nothing but the lessons and source of strength in disguise.

JANUARY 28

"When you affirm big, believe big and pray big, big things happen" Norman Vincent Peale

*Great things happen to those who hanker after
the greatest and never settle for less.*

You ought to dream big in order to reach somewhere along the lines of great. And if you by accident achieved the greatest, then the world becomes your stage. The thing about picking small and convenient goals is that you tend to land in the mediocre region.

JANUARY 29

"Example is not the main thing influencing others. It is the only thing" Albert Schweitzer

Examples are the only healthy influence.

For those who have come before us, have left their names carved in the sands of time for us to look up to their approaches. It is always a good idea to have an inspiration to follow as it shows you from where to start.

JANUARY 30

"The best things in life are yours if you can appreciate yourself" DC

"Self-love begets you to treat yourself with the best."

You have to love yourself if you want others to love you. The love has to begin from you, and the same is the case with self-respect. The way you treat yourself is exactly the way others are going to treat you. So be kind to yourself and others will be kind to you.

JANUARY 31

"Keep going, someone must be on top, why not you" George Patton

"Aim for the highest of degree as someone ought to get that position."

Someone is going the take the position their position in the topmost business; it can be you too if you strive like a mad man. It only looks like a dream when you are really far from it, but it becomes achievable when you are determined to reach that position.

FEBRUARY 1

"Let us never negotiate out of fear but let us never fear to negotiate"
John F Kennedy

Negotiate as it has never been negotiated before.

S uch is the rule of life. if you want to swim in the ocean, you have to let go of the fear of drowning. If you want to do air gliding, you ought to do without the fear of heights. In the same way, if you dream of winning a project, you should have the skills to negotiate. All you are supposed to do is put the relevant pointers and talk with validity.

FEBRUARY 2

"Feeling gratitude and not expressing it is like wrapping a present and not giving it." — William Arthur Ward, Scholar

Gratitude is only executed when expressed.

I f you feel, someone has gone out of their way to help you out; then you are obliged to show gratitude towards them. It costs nothing but two kind words to let someone know what it meant to you and how it made you feel. Gratitude is best fitted for two places, your heart and on your tongue.

FEBRUARY 3

"Genius is one percent inspiration, ninety-nine percent perspiration" Thomas Alva Edison

One of the most geniuses who've ever set foot on earth were the ones who sweat their rust in achieving the purpose.

N othing great can be ever be achieved without breaking a sweat in pursuit of getting it. The energy you put into making a dream come true is the energy best employed. If you search, you're going to find that all the successful men who've ever stayed on earth have had a way of striving till it sweats, as they believed sweat is the luckiest for a man in making.

FEBRUARY 4

"When angry, count to 10 before you speak; if very angry, count to 100" Thomas Jefferson

> *It is required of an individual to think a thousand times before speaking when angry.*

S ince ages, ferociousness has always done man bad. It makes him lose his mind and spit venom onto anyone they didn't intend and blurt out things that only hurt. And the worst of all, it brings regrets later as you ought to lose some real friends in the process. This is why it's always essential to look before you leap and maintain your silence when angry.

FEBRUARY 5

"Decide upon your Dreams and Goals: Write down your specific goals and develop a plan to reach them" (from IBD's 10 secrets to success)

> *Hunt your soul to extract a purpose, list down your dreams, and then execute.*

I t is required of a person who is in search of himself to sit down, reflect and dig down their soul. The purpose sits right there, waiting to be unveiled by you. And if you find difficulty in finding it, then think about the times when your mind conjured a 'what if' as a possibility on your worst days. That what-if is precisely your purpose. Next thing, you know what to do.

FEBRUARY 6

"Take Action: Goals are nothing without action. Don't be afraid to get started. Just do it" from IBD's 10 secrets to success.

Dream and then work toward achieving it
without the fear of being judged.

For those who keep thinking about the mundane task of fitting in couldn't go any further than the crowd. As for those who don't pay heed to the norms and opinions and dream about the universe, they end up somewhere among the stars. So, it's better to let go of the fear of criticism and start pursuing your dream.

FEBRUARY 7

"Never stop learning: Go back to school or read books. Get training and acquire skills" from IBD's 10 secrets to success.

The process of learning should never stop regardless
of the age, gender, and circumstances of a person.

There is no age of learning. The barriers are only in mind. The learning phase should last a lifetime as in that way; your mind never grows old. A mind that stores the treasure of information and still keeps feeding on knowledge never grows old and weary.

FEBRUARY 8

"Be persistent and work hard: Success is a marathon, not a sprint. Never give up" from IBD's 10 secrets to success.

*Hard work and consistency are the keys
to achieve any milestone in life.*

C onsistency is a talent that only a few are bestowed with, not everyone can practice it. For those who do, achieve little by little every day. And is exactly how they achieve big things in life by taking one step toward their goals. Let consistency be the key and watch as success kisses your feet.

FEBRUARY 9

"If they can do it, why can't I?" Saint Augustine, wrote this for the inspiration of the self for excellence, happiness, and fulfillment in God.

This is also true for the inspiration of the self for achieving success in our life. Successful people like Bill Gates of Microsoft, Steve Jobs of Apple, Jeff Bezos of Amazon were ordinary people who achieved extraordinary success because of their dedication and hardwork in pursuit of their vision and goals. A great idea can make you a billionaire if you are able to conceive it, nourish it, plan it, and execute your plan with dedication and focus.

Whatever you plan on doing and achieving, perform it today.

I f you have a dream, start working on it today. The pursuit of dreams should be void of putting the tasks aside for tomorrows and instead be focused on beginning today. It's the todays that constitute our tomorrow.

FEBRUARY 10

"Learn to analyze details: get all facts, all the input. Learn from your mistakes" from IBD's 10 secrets to success.

It is wise to gather all the details, jot down all the relevant pointers, look into your mistakes, and then work toward it.

M istakes are the wisest teacher if you look close enough. What a sensible man does is he puts down all of his mistakes in a paper and clip it to his cupboard to give him a reminder of what shouldn't be done again.

FEBRUARY 11

"Focus your time and money: Don't let other people or things distract you" from IBD's 10 secrets to success.

Stay focused and invest your money; don't let the distractions affect you.

I f you have a dream to work on, start working. Revolve your entire world around this one point of focus and stay committed to it. If your dream requires your financial investment, give that too. Give all of what you have and don't distract yourself.

FEBRUARY 12

"Don't be afraid to innovate; be different: Following the herd is a sure way to mediocrity" from IBD's 10 secrets to success.

Come up with ideas and innovations. It's better to stand out than to worry about the mundane task of fitting in.

F or those who worry about fitting in, live for the satisfaction of others but not themselves. By the time they reach adult age, they have lots of unlived days and unfulfilled dreams. In that way, they spend the rest of their lives filled with regrets over the unutilized time.

FEBRUARY 13

"Deal and communicate with people effectively: No person is an island. Learn to understand and motivate others" from IBD's 10 secrets to success.

Listen to experienced people for they have
something important to say.

Every person has something important to tell you. Communicate and listen carefully. Exchange a word of motivation every now and then if possible.

FEBRUARY 14

"Be honest and dependable; Take responsibility; Otherwise, Nos 1-9 won't matter" from IBD's 10 secrets to success.

He, who doesn't have responsibilities on his
shoulders, is the most careless of the kind.

Not everyone can bear responsibilities for it takes energy, concern, and wealth of a person. Out of the lot of some really responsible men, there exists a reckless lot. A herd that is only concern about himself and his peace of life. And humans deem them the most useless boulder on earth.

FEBRUARY 15

"If a man hasn't discovered something that he will die for, he isn't fit to live" Martin Luther King

A man has to have a purpose of living
lucid to him in order to survive.

W hat purpose is to living is what destination is to the traveler. Without a sense of direction as to where you're wandering, you can never reach anywhere, let alone find a home. One has to have a purpose laid out before him to have something to follow and look up to.

FEBRUARY 16

"Plan your work for today and every day, then work your plan" Norman Vincent Peale

The successes of life are defined by how many days have you invested in planning your today, tomorrow and day after tomorrow.

O ne must have a planning structure to work on as to what are their productive plans for today, what should be done per hour and then it goes to the same planning for tomorrow, structured hour by hour. And then it should extend to the day after tomorrow till it reaches a point where a person starts wondering where does he see himself 5 years from now.

FEBRUARY 17

"Develop success from failures. Discouragement and failure are two of the surest stepping stones to success" Dale Carnegie

Learn from your failures as they are the building blocks of success.

F ail. Fail miserably. But get back up again. Try till all your wrongs turn right. Till your sweat turn to dust, and you learn from your failures. Once learned, make it a way to never look back and learn from your mistakes.

FEBRUARY 18

"In the middle of difficulty lies opportunity" Albert Einstein

Opportunity knocks when you aren't looking.

W ant an adventure? Go into a tunnel if you can. Stay there till your adventure turns into horror. Hold on a little longer till all your hopes are lost. Wait a little longer and stop expecting and see as a beam of light only comes from the end of the tunnel because it only comes when you aren't looking.

FEBRUARY 19

"The best executive is the one who has sense enough to pick good men to do what he wants done, and self-restraint enough to keep from meddling with them while they do it" Theodore Roosevelt

Mark of a leader is that he recruits wisely, get the desired work done, and don't unnecessarily nags his people.

A leader knows when to push when to strike and how to get things done their side. He doesn't unnecessarily bug his people and chit chat about their lives.

FEBRUARY 20

"Yesterday is the past. Tomorrow is the future. Today is a gift and that's why we call it the present." "He who dares nothing need hope for nothing." "Far better is it to dare mighty things, to win glorious triumphs - even though checkered by failure - than to rank with those poor spirits who neither enjoy much nor suffer much, because they live in a gray twilight that knows not victory nor defeat." — Theodore Roosevelt

*There is a reason why the past is in the
past, and the present is a present.*

Never dwell on your past, for the present always has something new to offer. You can only expect the great outcome after giving your best input. Trying out bigger thing never does anybody any harm as failing is the opportunity to learn and triumphing is the fruit itself. It's always a great idea to give it a try.

FEBRUARY 21

"We must combine the toughness of the serpent and the softness of the dove, a tough mind and a tender heart" Martin Luther King.

*Anyone who can muster two opposite traits in a skillful
manner can understand the colors of life better.*

A man who can skillfully manage two of his traits is a man who can manage anything in life. The greatest art is to be able to manage your emotions and only let the suitable one out as per the situation.

FEBRUARY 22

"We tend to get what we expect" Norman Vincent Peale

*Good breeds forth good, bad engenders bad.
It all depends on what we anticipate.*

You tend to get what you expect. Good thoughts are going to yield good outcomes. Bad thoughts are automatically going to generate bad results. Our thought process plays a vital role in developing a situation – good or bad in our minds and then later becomes our realties.

FEBRUARY 23

"Become a possibilitarian. No matter how dark things seem to be or actually are, raise your sights and see possibilities-always see them, for they're always there. Norman Vincent Peale

Hold on! The good only comes after the bad.

There is always light after the dark, joy after sorrow, pain after relief, and strength after weakness. It's unto humans to keep their faith strong and get going.

FEBRUARY 24

"When you affirm big, believe big and pray big, big things happen" Norman Vincent Peale

Aim big to achieve big. Aim small and weep over the small.

When you wish to achieve big things, you end up achieving something along the lines of great. Whereas, when you aim for the conveniently achievable things, then you land within the boundary of mediocre.

FEBRUARY 25

Any fact facing us is not as important as our attitude toward it, for that determines our success or failure. Norman Vincent Peale

Attitude matters more than behavior because it is the determinant variable of one's success or failure.

Everything begins and ends with attitude. With the right one, you can reach heights. With the incorrect one, you stay where you are. If you have the right attitude toward success, no power on earth can stop you from achieving it.

FEBRUARY 26

"You're only as good as the people you hire" Ray Kroc

The proficiency of the people you hire reflects your own mastery.

While recruiting, you tend to look for qualities that you either yourself have or look up to have. If either of the criteria is matched, you end up hiring the individual. This is why you are accountable and responsible for the people you recruit.

FEBRUARY 27

"Example is not the main thing influencing others. It is the only thing" Albert Schweitzer.

That is the thing about examples; they live on forever even if the human dies.

Great men who have come before us have done something that is still remembered. And that is why we want to leave our name in the sands of time because it remains even after a thousand years later.

FEBRUARY 28

"The quality of an individual is reflected in the standards they set for themselves "Ray Kroc

If you ever want to judge a person values and virtues, look for what principles he sets for himself.

A man has to have a rule book and a certain set of principle for himself. Righteous is the man who sets for himself the same principle that he imposes on others.

MARCH 1

"Beware of little expenses. A small leak can sink a great ship" Benjamin Franklin.

It's the little things that build up to make big differences.

L ife is really beautiful, and it is because of those small things on which if we focus and work hard toward, it can turn out to be sublime, and if we ignore, we can make things difficult for us. It is in the same way how a bird collects small, inconsequential things in its beak to make a nest for its little ones.

MARCH 2

"There is no higher religion than human service. To work for the common good is the greatest creed". Albert Schweitzer

Philanthropy is the only religion I believe in and practice. There is no other greater good in this world than kindness and generosity.

P hilanthropy is an act of charity which eliminates a social problem. For me, there is no good charity then the charity of kindness and helping people by providing them with a healthy environment to live in. It is what I do and believes in.

MARCH 3

"We hold these truths to be self-evident: that all men are created equal; that they are endowed by their creator with certain unalienable rights; that among these are life, liberty, and the pursuit of happiness" Thomas Jefferson

If there is one thing that aligns us all, it's that we all are going through one shift of day and night we call life.

L ife doesn't stop for anyone. Everyone is living it as if we all are in this vehicle of life, waiting for this journey to end. Everyone has different destinations, goals, crisis, we are traveling for our own cause, but we all are riding in this vehicle, which we all call 'life.'

MARCH 4

"The height of your accomplishments will equal the depth of your convictions." — William F. Scolavino

The higher the altitude of your accomplishments, the deeper the pit of your understanding and belief.

I f a person is really successful in his life, the success is not a miracle; what he has learned from his life experience and failure, that is a miracle. This is why it is said that an old person has more knowledge and deep understanding of life because he has spent a lifetime learning from his experiences and failures.

MARCH 5

"A mind always employed is always happy. This is true secret, the grand recipe, for felicity". Thomas Jefferson

You ought to keep your mind busy and functioning because, in that way, no evil or bizarre thought can cross your mind.

O ne should always keep oneself busy in doing some work so that he doesn't have free time to think and focus on things which are unnecessary. For example, if a person has a lot of work to do, he doesn't have time to go through his Instagram and surf hours on the internet just for entertainment which isn't helpful in practical life either.

MARCH 6

"The care of human life and happiness, and not their destruction, is the first and only legitimate object of good government" Thomas Jefferson

An exemplary government ensures the betterment and well-being of their people and assures the safest of operations.

A government has a fair idea of what its people want. It operates in a manner that serves the good of people. An effective government is all aware of what measures to be taken for both the economic status and long-term well-being of its people.

MARCH 7

"The most valuable of all talents is that of never using two words when one will do" Thomas Jefferson.

It's better to utter one word of wisdom than to blabber two words of utter bullshit.

A wise man once said that when a person talks, he must use good and kind words, as good and kind words don't ever hurt anyone and helps him make a soft corner in the hearts of others whereas a person who talks rubbish do not have any respect.

MARCH 8

"When angry, count to 10 before you speak; if very angry, count to 100" Thomas Jefferson

Anger has the habit of getting the best of you. Don't allow it.

E veryone gets angry, and it is a very strong emotion that doesn't only cause damage to others but all of us. There are lots of friendships which ended due to anger. As when angry, you don't realize most of what you are saying; you just want to take out your frustration which sometimes results in losing your loved ones.

MARCH 9

"I am a great believer in luck, and I find the harder I work the more I have of it" Thomas Jefferson

Hard work always pays off. The harder you work,
the more you advance toward success.

There is no effort that goes in vain. There is always a time when you see that the efforts you put in are working for you.

MARCH 10

"One man practicing sportsmanship is far better than a hundred teaching it" Knute Rockne

Practical implementation is a lot better than a verbal suggestion.

An old person has a good sense and piece of advice related to how to live a successful life because he has had an experience of a lifetime. When we give our younger siblings a lesson for life, they don't understand as they haven't gone through a situation, they haven't lived it. That is why practicality is a lot better than verbal suggestions.

MARCH 11

"Heaven will be inherited by every man who has heaven in his soul" Confucius

He, who has a good sense of virtue, carries
heaven everywhere he goes.

W hen a person has a good heart and has moral values, then it doesn't matter wherever he goes, he will leave the marks of his good deeds everywhere. He will remember that he has to do good and will never forget his vision of living.

MARCH 12

"We must build a new world, a far better world-one in which the eternal dignity of man is respected" Harry S Truman.

Every human desire to construct a world for himself,
where he could live with respect and dignity.

R espect and dignity are what every human desire in this world. Every human wants to be respected for his work, opinion, and anything he does.

MARCH 13

"Get a good idea and stay with it. Dog it, and work at it until it's done, and done right" Walt Disney

Brainstorm an idea, formulate the structure,
and then work towards it.

O ne should come up with an amazing idea that also serves for the betterment of this world. Next step is to prepare its structure methodically and work hard in implementing it. Like a group of young university students built a mega project to provide electricity in rural areas.

MARCH 14

"All our dreams can come true-if we have the courage to pursue them" Walt Disney.

"All our dreams can come true if we have the courage to pursue them."

Everyone struggles to make his dream come true, but they give up on their dreams when things begin to go wrong. What in fact you need to remember is that nothing can hinder you from achieving your goals if you really stick by them. Like how the Prime Minister of Pakistan Imran Khan made all his dreams come true after years of struggle.

MARCH 15

"Associate yourself with men of good quality if you esteem your own reputation, for 'tis better to be alone than in bad company" George Washington

Surround yourself with great people as we tend to pick the influence quickly.

The people we surround ourselves with are the ones we get influenced by. So, make sure you have good people around you who are constantly vibing positive energy.

MARCH 16

"Do not do tomorrow what you can do today. If you feel the need to forgive, forgive today. If you feel the need to risk, risk today. If you feel the need to apologize, apologize today. If you feel the need to love someone, love them today. If you feel the need to create something, create something today. If you do this there will be no conflict within, you will grow in Spirit because you will be your true authentic Self - living at full potential. Live today not for tomorrow." —Wallace Huey

Whatever you plan on doing and achieving, perform it today.

I f you have a dream, start working on it today. The pursuit of dreams should be void of putting the tasks aside for tomorrows and instead be focused on beginning today. It's the todays that constitute our tomorrow.

MARCH 17

"The difference between an educated and uneducated man is the same difference as between being alive and being dead" Aristotle

What distinguishes a literate man from an illiterate one is that one is wakeful to the realities of life while the other is blinded.

A sensible and literate person is well aware of the realities of life and is experienced while the illiterate person goes around without having a reality check.

MARCH 18

"Education is the best provision for old age" Aristotle.

The old can always count on and return to education as the only best asset for their exhausted mind.

E ducation is the best asset possessed by a human being. Even as you grow old, there is still enough capacity in your mind to accept information if you have spent your entire life in a healthy habit of reading.

MARCH 19

"Beauty is the gift of God" Aristotle.

The greatest blessing of God is the beauty descended on earth.

But one of the best gifts to mankind from God is nature's beauty. No wonder Earth is occupied by countless bounties of nature.

MARCH 20

"Nature does nothing uselessly" Aristotle

Nature is never void of purpose.

Every creature on this planet is made to serve a purpose. Like trees provide oxygen and the houseflies help in pollination. Similarly, every creature is designed to serve a purpose.

"MARCH 21

"Well begun is half done" Aristotle.

If the start is good, the end is worth it.

If the things are under control at the start of anything, then surely it will end well too.

MARCH 22

"The weak can never forgive. Forgiveness is the attribute of the strong" Mahatma Gandhi.

The mere act of forgiveness is only conducted by the
emotionally strong. The weak can't afford to lend this gift.

T he stronger you are, the more forgiving you will be. Holding a grudge weakens your inner strength, so it's better to forgive.

MARCH 23

"Honest differences are often a healthy sign of progress" Mahatma Gandhi

It's better to have honest and up-front arguments
than backstabs and vague differences.

Y ou should surround yourself with people who are blunt and straight-forward rather than the people who pretend to agree with you but backstab later.

MARCH 24

"Anger dwells only in the bosom of fools" Albert Einstein.

Outrage and ill-temperament are only the languages of fools.

D on't lose your temper quickly because that is what fools do. Instead, be mature and react as per the situation in a humble way.

MARCH 25

The impossible is often the untried." —Jim Goodwin

Nothing is impossible. The hurdles and
obstacles are always in our mind.

Don't let your fears stop you from what you want to do. Everything can be achieved if you make it happen. And you can overcome every obstacle until you don't let your fears in mind overshadow you.

MARCH 26

"You never achieve real success unless you like what you are doing" Dale Carnegie.

You have to be passionate about what you're doing;
otherwise, there is no point in doing that activity.

Do what you love and love what you do! Simply adopt the profession and work you like and do it with all your heart and power. Otherwise its useless putting efforts in the field you have no interest in.

MARCH 27

"Nothing is particularly hard if you divide it into small jobs" (Henry Ford)

Divide the complex tasks into simple pieces
and continue working on one at a time.

Don't work in parallel on complex tasks. It will give zero output. Instead, break it into simple small tasks and work on them individually to give the maximum output.

MARCH 28

"You know we don't grow most of the food we eat. We wear clothes other people make. We speak a language that other people developed. We use a mathematics that other people evolved... I mean, we're constantly taking things. It's a wonderful, ecstatic feeling to create something that puts it back in the pool of human experience and knowledge." —Steve Jobs

It's ironic how we are living on borrowed bones.
Without trade, we wouldn't have survived.

W e are living on things which we haven't worked for ourselves. We eat what isn't harvested by us, wear what isn't designed or stitched by us, speak a language which isn't invented by us. It's funny how we are always chucking on the fruits sowed by someone else.

MARCH 29

"Coming together is a beginning; keeping together is progress; working together is success" Henry Ford.

There is a start in gathering for a purpose. Progress in sticking
together and success in working towards achieving a goal.

I f we start something for a purpose and stick by it no matter how many obstacles come in our way, strive for it with our team, then surely one-day success will make its way.

MARCH 30

"Don't find fault. Find a remedy" Henry Ford

Look for solutions instead of faults.

We should learn from our mistakes and make way for solutions by considering it as an experience. Instead of focusing on the faults.

MARCH 31

"If a man has done his best, what else is there?" George Patton

*If you've given your best and served your best on
the plate, there is nothing else that matters.*

If you have worked really hard and you're satisfied with all the efforts you put in, then you would have no regrets, and that is what matters.

APRIL 1

"There is no security in this life, only opportunity" Douglas Macarthur

He, who dare not step out of the comfort zone, never
witnesses the opportunity knocking his door.

You should not hesitate to work anywhere. One should be daring and challenging enough to work out of one's comfort zone when necessary in order to avail a certain opportunity.

APRIL 2

"It is fatal to enter any war without the will to win it" Douglas Macarthur

He, who dreads the war, never wins it.

Never fear the challenges you come across in order to achieve something. Because if those fears overshadow your vision, you will never achieve it.

APRIL 3

"In the central place of every heart there is a recording chamber. So long as it receives a message of beauty, hope, cheer, and courage-so long are you young. When the wires are all down and our heart is covered with the snow of pessimism and the ice of cynicism, then, and only then, are you grown old. (Douglas Macarthur)

Our heart happens to store everything it witnesses and hears.

Our heart's well-being and healthy state are highly dependent on the message of love, hope and the valor it receives. The system breaks down, and you turn old when it's fed with the message of hate and despair.

APRIL 4

"Ability may get you to the top, but it takes character to keep you there" John wooden.

Not everyone can withstand failure, and not everyone can enjoy the glory of success.

A nyone can reach the top with the talent and abilities they have, but it requires the greatest of characters to stay there.

APRIL 5

"Failure to prepare is preparing to fail" John Wooden

One should be ready and prepared for all the thick and thins. Otherwise, they will fail miserably.

B efore taking a risk, one should be all prepped up for all the consequences. There is no point in quitting midway which brings nothing but regrets of 'should have held a bit longer.'

APRIL 6

"Anyone who stops is old, whether at 20 or 80. Anyone who keeps learning stays young. The greatest thing in life is to keep your mind young" Henry ford.

There is no restricted age to learning and education if you're an enthusiast.

N o matter what your age is, the important thing is to keep your mind young. And you should always keep learning and moving forward to keep yourself active.

APRIL 7

"Failure is only the opportunity to begin again more intelligently"
Henry Ford

Failure introduces you to a hundred ways
of not doing a task that way.

N ever lose hope if you fail once. Instead, take it as an experience, learn from it, and keep going.

APRIL 8

"If money is your hope for independence, you will never have it. The only real security that a man can have in this world is a reserve of knowledge, experience and ability" Henry Ford

For those who chase after money to have a liberal
life, can never have it. But for those who seek wisdom
through education attain real security in his life.

O nly your knowledge, ability, and experience can help you with the dealings of life, and that resides in you. No money and materialistic goods can help you with it.

APRIL 9

"It is not the employer who pays the wages-he only handles the money. It is the product that pays wages" Henry Ford

It is only the quality of product and services
that bring a business good fortune.

I f the services provided by the company will be worth it, then the consumers will spend money on them easily with their will without the extra efforts put by the employer to generate sales.

Therefore, your product must be of good quality to convince consumers not your dealing.

APRIL 10

"Football games are generally won by the boys with the greatest desire" Paul Bryant

> *He, who is resolved to win, wins – be it the*
> *Olympic Games or battle of life.*

A person who is passionate enough about his victory and works hard day and night towards its goals and achievement is the one who comes up as winner at the end of the day. Therefore, in order to achieve something, you need to put in all your energy and efforts.

APRIL 11

"Accept the challenges so that you may feel the exhilaration of victory" George Patton

> *The true essence of victory is felt after*
> *fighting with it all your power.*

If you work with full devotion without hesitating from the obstacles that might come across, then you will enjoy its outcome with full enthusiasm.

APRIL 12

"Wars may be fought with weapons, but they are won by men. It is the spirit of the men who follow and of the man who leads that gains the victory" George Patton

Battles aren't won with weapons; they are won with vim and vigor.

Wars might be fought with the help of advanced weapons, but that is not the factor for a soldier's victory but the spirit to win is. It is only a person's dedication and enthusiasm that goes as an input for a successful output.

APRIL 13

"The most vital quality a soldier can possess is self-confidence" George Patton

He who wears the masks of wise and speaks with convictions, the world is his to conquer.

Self-confidence and self-worth is the most important key to win a war and achieve a goal.

APRIL 14

"You must be single minded. Drive for the one thing on which you have decided" George Patton

Once you made your mind for something, then stick to it and do not confuse yourself with various thoughts.

For those who have multiple things going on in their mind cannot think straight. It is essential to be single-minded and take one task at a time.

APRIL 15

"If you are going to win any battle you have to do one thing. You must make the mind run the body. Never let the body tell the mind what to do" George Patton

The quality of the resolved and determined men is that they never let exhaustion to hinder their vision.

I f you take up any task and decide to work upon it, then work on it with full devotion using your mind. And do not give up mid-way even if you're tired and exhausted. Then surely you will make your way to success soon.

APRIL 16

"Keep going, someone must be on top, why not you." George Patton

There is an empty slot on the top, and it should be taken by you.

W hen others can succeed through hard work and dedication, then you can succeed too. You should keep on going until you reach that position.

APRIL 17

"Look ahead of you, never behind. Have faith in yourself. If you do, you will be amazed at what you can accomplish" T.L Nash

For those who believe in themselves can surpass the threshold.

A lways keep moving forward and do not regret past mistakes. Focus on your potential and discover your hidden talent, then you would love to see the output of your abilities.

APRIL 18

"Don't ever forget that you are unique.
Be your best self
And not an imitation of someone else.
Find your strengths,
And use them in positive way.
Don't listen to those who question the choices you make.
Travel the road that you have chosen,
And don't look back with regret.
Remember that there is plenty of time
To travel another road-
And still another-
In your journey through life.
Take the time to find the route that is right for you"
Jacqueline Schiff

We all are unique in our ways.

B e your best self. And not an imitation of someone else. Find your strengths and use them in a positive way. Don't listen to those who question the choices you make. Travel the road that you have chosen and don't look back with regret. Remember that there is plenty of time to travel another road- And still another in your journey through life. Take the time to find the route that is right for you.

APRIL 19

"Every morning you are handed twenty-four golden hours. They are some of the few things in this world that you get free of charge. If you had all the money in the world, you couldn't buy an extra hour. What will you do with this precious treasure? – author unknown.

Each day brings you a gift of another twenty-four golden
hours. There nothing that can't be done in this plenty of time.
Utilize your time wisely and make the most of each hour.

Time is the most precious thing. Once it is gone, it will never come back, no money and no wealth can bring you moments which you didn't utilize. Therefore, don't spend all your life in making money only. Spend your time wisely, make the most of each second gifted to you.

APRIL 20

"Life is an ever-changing process, and nothing is final. Therefore, each moment and every new day is a chance to begin anew" Barbara Cage

What feels like the end isn't, in fact, an end.
You can begin again tomorrow.

If something bad happens it's not permanent and similarly good is temporary too. Therefore, don't give up on any point. Grab every chance coming your way every day to avail new opportunities and keep going.

APRIL 21

"The just act as guides to their neighbors, but the way of wicked leads them astray" Proverbs of Solomon (12-28)

There are plenty of good people in this world who are
going to navigate the right direction for you but beware
the wicked! For they are there to send you off the rails.

Good people take advice from their friends and guide them to the correct path, but an evil person is easily led to do wrong and led others to the wrong path.

APRIL 22

"I am not discouraged, because every wrong attempt discarded is another step forward" Thomas a. Edison.

*Even the wrong paths teach you about the
paths that shouldn't be taken.*

Y ou should not hesitate to step back from anything wrong even if you are mid-way, because it might seem that you're moving backward, but the elimination of something wrong is actually a step forward towards betterment.

APRIL 23

"A wise son gives his father joy, but a foolish son is a grief to his mother. Proverbs of Solomon (Chapter 10-1) The New American Bible.

*A well-raised is a source of pride, but a folly
one brings nothing but misery.*

A loving and caring son is a wise man, and he never let his parents down. He finds ways to make them happy and proud. Parents should be one's first priority. On the other hand, the one who makes his parents sad is a fool person because he will regret it later.

APRIL 24

"The mouth of the just is a fountain of life, but the mouth of wicked conceals violence" Proverbs of Solomon (10-2)

*A man of justice only speaks for the betterment of
people, but an evil man only thinks about himself.*

A just person will always speak the truth, and his words will bring positive change in others. But a wicked person never expresses his true thoughts. His words will never show what he has in his heart.

APRIL 25

"The wise store up knowledge, but the mouth of a fool is imminent ruin" Proverbs of Solomon (10-14)

The wise only speaks words of wisdom but
a fool only blabbers and rants.

A wise person speaks up the truth and gives suggestions from his vast knowledge and experience to others. And on the other hand, a fool utters nothing sensible and doesn't have anything to offer to others.

APRIL 26

"It is the Lord's blessing that brings wealth, and no effort can substitute it" Proverbs of Solomon

If the wealth is written in your fate, you'll get it no matter
what. If it isn't, no amount of energy can bring it for you.

I f you are blessed with anything in life, it's only because of God's blessings upon you and nothing from any other source. So always be humble and thankful to God for whatever he has bestowed upon you.

APRIL 27

"When the tempest passes, the wicked are no more; but the just are established forever" Proverbs of Solomon (10-25)

When a storm is over, all that is left is the examples of the righteous man; the wicked are never remembered.

Y ou ought to make your brief stay on earth worthwhile by serving humanity so that when you die, you leave a mark. The wicked are so doomed that neither is his life worthwhile, nor is his death.

APRIL 28

"It is better to dwell in a corner of the house than in a mansion with a quarrelsome woman" Proverbs of Solomon (21,9)

To live with a virtuous wife in a small cottage is a lot better than living with a sinful wife in a castle.

I t is important to bring a wife of virtue than a wife of beauty. A good woman makes a house a better place to live in. You can have all the luxuries of life, but if you don't have a pious wife, all your earning goes in vain. A virtuous wife is always satisfied even if you keep her in a small cottage and a wicked wife is never content even if you feed her pure honey.

APRIL 29

"To find a wife is to find happiness, a favor granted by the Lord" Proverbs of Solomon (18-22)

A good wife is the blessing of God.

I f you have found your true love in a woman who is your wife, then that's the greatest blessing of Lord upon you. A loving wife will fill your life with happiness.

APRIL 30

"Fools immediately show their anger, but the shrewd conceal contempt" Proverbs of Solomon (12-16)

The wise sips down his anger, whereas a fool burst out. And judgmental is the worst of all as he conceals contempt in his heart.

Don't get triggered easily and never show your anger on worthless issues; only fools do that. A wise person will not pay heed to small issues and never let their anger take over them in front of others.

MAY 1

"The heart of the intelligent acquires knowledge, and the ear of the wise seeks knowledge" Proverbs of Solomon (18-15)

Surround yourself with the wise to learn in every step of your life.

A wise person always prefers to surround himself with the wise and hear words of wisdom. An intelligent person seeks out the company of the wise to enlighten himself with knowledge. And in this way, the wisdom is imparted.

MAY 2

"Those who spare their words are truly knowledgeable, and those who are discreet are intelligent" Proverbs of Solomon (17-27)

Smart is the man who maintains his low-profile despite knowledge. Wise is the man who circulates his wisdom.

W hoever chooses to speak a lot and impart his wisdom is highly educated, but those who stay low-key despite the wisdom are intelligent. Wisdom is meant to get across before it reaches the grave and rot.

MAY 3

"No amount of straining, crying, or agonizing can remake one single day of the year that is past. But a little careful planning and thoughtful working out can make many glorious days in the future" (unknown author.

Only fools can live in the past. But wise prepare for the future.

D welling in the past could bring nothing but wails, sobs, and regret. Planning each hour of the present prepares you for heydays of the future.

MAY 4

"The plans of the diligent end in profit, but those of the hasty end in loss" Proverbs of Solomon (21-5)

Those who plan vigilantly and thoughtfully are successful, whereas those who rush in panic are in utter loss.

Panicking about a situation doesn't alleviate the problem an inch but in fact, makes it worse. Calm is a superpower that only a few can have in the middle of adversity. It's a talent to maintain their nerves in the midst of chaos.

MAY 5

"Those who guard their mouths preserve themselves, those who open wide their lips bring ruin" Proverbs of Solomon (13-3)

For those who maintain their silence are in less trouble than those who speak a lot.

For the one who speaks less isn't as much in trouble than the one who speaks more. You tend not to do justice to the people by speaking a lot and giving away their secrets. As the more you speak, the more links are you going to leak relevant to the secrets of others.

MAY 6

"Wealth won quickly dwindles away, but gathered little by little, it grows" Proverbs of Solomon (13-11)

A hefty amount of wealth goes away as quickly as it comes.

A wealth that comes quickly and in bulk doesn't last long, but the wealth gathered little by little make up a good fortune if the only one remembers to save.

MAY 7

"The teachings of the wise is a fountain of life, turning one from the snares of death" Proverbs of Solomon (13-14)

The wise are always the best guide. Through intuition, they can save you from the mouth of death.

That is the thing about wise men; they don't beat you with experience but wisdom. Their intuition is stronger than rest and sixth sense more vigilant than a tiger. Beware! If he warns you about something, expect the danger is approaching.

MAY 8

"Whoever spares the rod hates the child, but whoever loves will apply discipline" Proverbs of Solomon (13-24)

Make your child discipline and watch as they succeed.

The great gift a parent can give to their children is discipline as it makes him a man of structure and vision. But parents who breeze blithely past the chaos of their child are their biggest enemy.

MAY 9

"The naïve believe everything, but the shrewd watch their steps" Proverbs of Solomon (14-15)

The sharp-witted plan their steps vigilantly, but the fools don't and tend to believe every information thrown their way.

The clever ones are fully aware not all the information that comes their way is true, so they don't believe it before confirming it. Whereas a fool is quick to believe any information without validifying it. And that is the biggest difference between the two.

MAY 10

"The good leave inheritance to their children's children, but the wealth of the sinner is stored up for the just" Proverbs of Solomon (13-22)

The righteous leaves the divine message of virtue when he dies while the sinner leaves nothing but the wealth that is distributed among the virtuous.

The good-doers leave examples for the forthcoming generation whereas the fortune left by the sinner comes to the use of the fair men. The virtuous are fully aware of what to leave as an example for the coming generation to follow, so they choose their paths and actions wisely. The sinner is always at a loss. He is neither capable of leaving example nor wealth.

MAY 11

"Plans fail when there is no counsel, but they succeed when advisers are many" Proverbs of Solomon (15-22)

The more people you have, the more diverse the ideas your company possesses.

The more people you recruit for your mission, the more are the chances of its triumphs as you get to hear a thousand different opinions on a single subject.

MAY 12

"A cheerful glance brings joy to the heart; good news invigorates the bones" Proverbs of Solomon (15-30)

One enchanting glimpse is enough to thaw out all the worries; one act of love can raise your spirits.

S mall acts of kindness can make the whole sea of difference. Smiling at a stranger who has had a bad day, making an old lady cross the road, carrying loads of grocery of a woman and all such acts of kindness and love can make the world a lot better place.

MAY 13

"The fear of the Lord is training for wisdom, and humility goes before honors" Proverbs of Solomon" (15-33)

*The wise fear the Lord and seeks out
wisdom and stay humble about it.*

A man of wisdom fears none but God as it is unto Him that he has to return. He is only on a hunt for more knowledge, experience, and wisdom as nothing else really matters. But the best of his traits happen to be his humbleness despite the knowledge.

MAY 14

"Entrust your works to the Lord, and your plans will succeed" Proverbs of Solomon (16-3)

Work hard, do your part, and leave the success unto God.

A human is only supposed to work as hard as he can to achieve his purpose and invest his energy to the fullest and leave the rest for God to do.

MAY 15

"How much better to get wisdom than gold!" Proverbs of Solomon (16-16)

Wisdom is more precious than gold.

It's ironic how we have made the currency as the most precious and sought-after entity when, in fact, it's nothing. The real treasure on earth is the man and his brains that are capable of doing wonders. If the wisdom of the man will be weighed against gold, it's the wisdom that's going to win.

MAY 16

"Gray hair is a crown of glory; it is gained by a life that is just" Proverbs of Solomon (16-31)

> *Only the dignified few reach the old age; the grey line of hair is a testament to having lived a complete life.*

The grey hair of a man is nothing but a roadmap of all the places he had been, a museum of all the experiences he has had and a testament of having witnessed all the seasons of life. The grey hair of a man is a glory in itself.

MAY 17

"Children's children are the crown of the elderly, and the glory of children is their parentage" Proverbs of Solomon (17-6)

> *Grandchildren are the greatest achievement of the grandparents, and their character is the biggest earning of their lives.*

All the grandparents have a special connection with their grandchildren. It's always a pleasure to watch your generation growing and blooming. Though it makes you feel old, the endless happiness goes beyond seams when the children turn out to be virtuous.

MAY 18

"A friend is a friend at all times, and a brother is born for the time of adversity" Proverbs of Solomon (17-17)

You can tell apart a brother from a friend by
witnessing the presence of one during your downfalls
and struggle of others to help you out.

Those who stand by you during your worst are your friends, but those who try to help you out of the worst are the traits of a brother. You can find brothers out of friends and friends out of brothers as life rolls on. Wish good on those who lend you a shoulder to cry but keep returning to those who are willing to take action to drive out your darkness.

MAY 19

"A good name is more desirable than great riches, and high esteem, than gold and silver" Proverbs of Solomon" (22-1).

No treasure on earth can compete with the
honor of self-respect and dignity.

The greatest earning of man is his self-respect and dignity. And wealth cannot buy any of it. If a man will realize the real value of dignity, he would rather spend his entire life, earning it rather than chasing wealth.

MAY 20

"The glory of the young is their strength, and the dignity of the old is gray hair" Proverbs of Solomon (20-29)

The young win with their strength and the
aged with their grey strand of hair.

The aged ones with the grey lining of hair but a decade of experience have superiority over the young who have all the energy but stand as a naivete.

MAY 21

"Rich and Poor have a common bond: the Lord is the maker of them all" Proverbs of Solomon (22,2)

All humans are united by the decree of God.

There are many things mutual between two humans, but the prominent of them stays the faith in God as the creator of us all.

MAY 22

"Golden apples in silver settings are words spoken at the proper time" Proverbs of Solomon (25,11)

Nine-tenths of wisdom is in speaking the
words of substance at the right time.

Not everybody is gifted with the power of spontaneity. Only a few have the right senses to come up with the right words at the right time. And it is these wise people who hold no regret of not delivering a point at a time when it was needed.

MAY 23

"Whoever answers before listening, theirs is folly and shame" Proverbs of Solomon (Chapter 18-13)

To all those who listen to respond mindlessly
are stupid and at a loss.

The mere reason that a man starts a conversation is for the other person to listen and come up with their opinion or suggestion over something. But the real tragedy is that some of us never listen, we only let it go from one ear and out the other. And all those who do this are at a loss as they can never learn from the experience of others let alone give a suggestion.

MAY 24

"Luxury is not befitting a fool; much less should a slave rule over princess" Proverbs of Solomon (19-10)
(10-2)

> *Luxury is not for a foolish person to enjoy; a*
> *slave can never reign over the king.*

God, Himself doesn't give nails to a bald man for he is going to harm himself. Similarly, the fool doesn't know how to handle luxury; he ends up doing the misemployed it for the greater wrong and exploits it with naivety. Which is why a human isn't bestowed beyond his potential.

MAY 25

"There are friends who bring ruin, but there are true friends more loyal than a brother" Proverbs of Solomon (18-24)

> *Out of a horde of friends who have ill-intention, some*
> *are sincerer and dearer than blood-related brothers.*

Some friends who spit venom behind our backs and pretend to be good on our faces are far worse than enemies. Whereas some friends who cannot bear a word against us, let alone not reveal, our secrets are far better than family.

MAY 26

"Home and possessions are an inheritance from parents, but a prudent wife is from the Lord" Proverbs of Solomon (19-14)

The house and other related belongings are the natural possessions given by a parent to a child on birth, but a virtuous character is the blessing of God.

P arents can only do enough for a child to give them enough food supply, a roof to cover their heads and good clothes to wear. But the rest of his settings are decided and written in the book of fate by God. Though the parents can raise their child well, yet they don't have control over their mind which often beats the conditioning over the arrival of tribulation and goes out to chase bigger evils of life. A man of character is both a blessing for his parents and his fraternity.

MAY 27

"The wise are more powerful than the strong, and the learned than the mighty, for by strategy war is waged, and victory depends on many counselors" Proverbs of Solomon (24-5,6)

All it takes is the right man for the right action.

I t takes an educated man to reign the country, strategic maneuver to plan out the situation, wise to impart the mode of action and warriors to defeat the enemy.

MAY 28

"Open your mouth in behalf of the mute, and for the rights of the destitute; open your mouth, judge justly, defend the needy and the poor" Sayings of king Lemuel (31-8,9)) New American Bible.

Of what good use is our tongue if not used to speak against the injustice, if not worked up in delivering kind words.

G od has given us the power of speech to raise our voices against all the brutalities and injustice going on in the world rather than commenting about the poor dressing sense or unhealthy lifestyle of people. You should utilize your tongue to rather speak kind words to mend a soul.

MAY 29

"Listen to your father who begot you, do not despise your mother when she is old" Proverbs of Solomon (23-22)

Always be kind to your parents who raised you up.

P arents are the only people you can blindly put your trust in. They are all about warmth and protection. When they die, you feel like a cloud of safety has left your sky and you are exposed and vulnerable to all the dark powers residing on earth. The void they left amidst the regret of having spent little time with them is unmatchable.

MAY 30

"Optimism is a strategy for making a better future. Because unless you believe that the future can be better, it's unlikely you will step up and take responsibility for making it so. If you assume that there's no hope, you guarantee that there will be no hope. If you assume that there is an instinct for freedom, that there are opportunities to change things, there is a chance you may contribute to making a better world. The choice is yours." —Noam Chomsky

Optimism is the second name of hope to which humans can cling in times of despair.

O ptimism is necessary as a ray of hope to tie the humans with it. It gives a trail to hang onto during the hardship, and without it, a human will never rise up out of the dark.

MAY 31

"The wicked flee though none pursue; but the just, like a lion are confident" Proverbs of Solomon (28-1)

Wrongdoers are often cowards, whereas righteous ones are the most courageous.

The vice always lives in his shell from the fear of being caught, and the righteous freely roam around the street. The act of wrong is mostly done in the pitch-black night because the evil-doer is a coward. Had he been courageous, he'd been roaming around the street openly.

JUNE 1

"For the protection of wisdom is as the protection of money; and knowledge is profitable because wisdom gives life to those who possess it" Proverbs of Solomon (7-12)

Wisdom and knowledge are more precious than money as it gives a man his self-respect and dignity.

N o amount of wealth can bring a man as much respect as his character. The goal of a man should always be to earn respect and maintain dignity because the money comes and goes but respect, when gone, never comes back ever.

JUNE 2

"For whoever is chosen among all the living has hope: A live dog is better off than a dead lion" Proverbs of Solomon (9-4)

So long as you live, you have hope.

E ven if you are undergoing a trauma, even if you're facing financial problems and even if you are in an abusive relationship, there is still hope. As long as you live, there is always hope for a better tomorrow. So, cling onto that hope that better days are awaiting you and you'll never fall prey to despair.

JUNE 3

"Enjoy life with the wife you love, all the days of the vain life granted you under the sun... anything you can turn you're your hand to, do with whatever power you have ; ... for death is certain to all... seize whatever opportunity one has to find joy, if God grants it" Proverbs of Solomon (9-9)

Live in today for there is no tomorrow.

S pend leisure time with your loved ones, bask in the shade of the sun, enjoy rainfall, and live all such little moments while you can. After all, none of us have much longer time here.

JUNE 4

"If the axe becomes dull, and the blade is not sharpened, then effort must be increased. But the advantage of wisdom is success" Proverbs of Solomon (10,10)

An ax needs to be sharpened, or the woodcutter
has to employee twice the energy.

A n ax needs regular blade sharpening to avoid the rust or else a human has to double the energy to cut the tree. Contrary to this, when a human doubles his effort without a weapon to achieve his goals, he attains wisdom.

JUNE 5

"All rivers flow to the sea, yet never does the sea become full" Book of Ecclesiastes (1-7) The New American Bible

The oceans is so complete, yet it accepts anything that falls on it.

T he epitome of the ocean's endless capacity is that it never fails to accept even the river that flows on it. Such should be the mindset of human while gaining an education. There is already enough capacity in our minds that more information will never make it full.

JUNE 6

"Wise people have eyes in their heads, but fools walk in darkness" Book of Ecclesiastes (2-14)

The wise can forecast a danger before it comes into action,
whereas the naïve are blinded to the bitter reality of life.

The wise can foresee any fluke coming because of his strong intuition and years of experience. He can always be counted on to give the right advice and warn you about the forthcoming danger. On the other hand, the naïve is blinded by the appeal of things and can never tell apart a rainbow from the storm.

JUNE 7

"Do not let anger upset your spirit, for anger lodges in the bosom of the fool" Book of Ecclesiastes (7-9)

A wise man never lets anger get the best of
him while a fool is always welcoming.

Anger is like a sandstorm which obscures the vision of mankind. The difference between the intelligent and fool is that the former one waits for his mud to settle while the latter panics and psyches up.

JULY 8

"Until we can manage time, we can manage nothing else."
— Peter F. Drucker, Author and Management Expert

So long as we practice time management,
nothing else needs to be fixed.

Time management is the most important habit that needs to be adopted so that you don't miss out the little joys in life and have plenty of time to enjoy them. In your routine, a deadline should be set for everything you do so that you develop a good sense of structure and discipline in life.

JUNE 9

"It takes as much energy to wish as it does to plan."

— Eleanor Roosevelt, Former First Lady

Planning requires as much input as dreaming or sometimes more.

It takes time to lay down your plan, strategize a maneuver, and then deliver. You have work on hour by hour dynamics to ensure the right planning. Dreaming is easy, but it takes energy and sweat to deliver.

JUNE 10

"Skill and confidence are an unconquered army."

— George Herbert, Priest

No power on earth can beat or turn down talent and confidence.
Because everyone is gifted with a different form of it.

Every human is gifted with unique traits. Even two exceptional writers are in no competition with one another because their writing style is different. Therefore, people shouldn't be compared, as everyone is gifted differently. Also, if the talent comes with a sense of confidence, it acts as a cherry on top.

JUNE 11

"To be successful, you have to be able to relate to people; they have to be satisfied with your personality to be able to do business with you and to build a relationship with mutual trust."

— George Ross, Star of The Apprentice with Donald Trump

In the flourishment of a business, interpersonal
skills of the creator count a lot.

W hen an employee is called for an interview in an organization, the very first thing he tends to notice the communication skills of the interviewer. Such is the significance of the interpersonal skills of an employer who is always selling himself. An employer can never get his work done through his employees without having the right way to communicate it to them.

JUNE 12

"When I thought I couldn't go on, I forced myself to keep going. My success is based on persistence, not luck. "

— Estee Lauder, entrepreneur

It takes nothing to dream but persistence
to go on in fulfilling your dream.

I t way easier to dream then to struggle in making it come true. In order to fulfill a dream, you ought to work with blood and sweat to achieve it. Most of what you need at all times is consistency to stay motivated and perseverance against all the odds.

JUNE 13

"I will study and prepare, and someday my opportunity will come."
Abraham Lincoln

We ought to keep our kitty bag ready and
seize when the opportunity knocks.

W e need to stay geared up for future opportunities even when they're out of sight. In this way, you don't have to start from scratch when the opportunity finally knocks and seize it immediately before giving it aforethought and getting your paperwork ready.

JUNE 14

"Knowing is not enough; we must apply. Wishing is not enough; we must do."

— Johann Wolfgang Von Goethe, Author

Knowledge is to no avail when isn't put across,
wishing too is in vain when we don't perform.

K nowledge is meant to be circulated for in that way it grows. It is the right of a naivete to be enlightened with the grace of education for in that way it passes down the heirdom. There is no gain in wishing without taking action toward it.

JUNE 15

"A Goal Without a Plan is Only a Wish" Antoine de saint – exupery – French writer

We ought to have a strategic maneuver relevant to our
goal, otherwise wishing is for no practical good.

W ishing is common to every human. Since ages, mankind has been dwelling and dreaming as it costs nothing. But only a few have shown the grit and vigor to come forward with the resolve to achieve it. The real courage lies in fathoming an action to achieve your goal.

JUNE 16

"It does not matter how slowly you go up, so long as you don't stop."

— Confucius, Philosopher

The pace doesn't matter when you keep going forward.

G od has set a time zone for everyone. One may succeed early, the other may succeed later, but the success does come to anyone who is taking a stride forward.

JUNE 17

"If you can find a path with no obstacles, it probably doesn't lead anywhere."

— Frank A. Clark

What comes easy isn't worth the achievement.

T hings that worth it isn't free. And free things aren't worth it. Hurdles teach you to cope with patience and perseverance. The hurdles and obstacles we come across are a blessing and a source of learning.

JUNE 18

"Don't let yesterday take up too much of today."

— Will Rogers, humorist

Don't look back at your ugly yesterday or they'll reign over your today.

E veryone encounters with bad experiences. But we should move on forgetting about it. And don't let the ugly past hinder your way for the future.

JUNE 19

"Never say no when a client asks for something, even if it is the moon. You can always try, and anyhow there is plenty of time afterward to explain that it was not possible."

— Cesar Ritz, hotelier

*A customer should never be refused of their demands
even if you ask you to fetch the moon.*

Build a good relationship with the customer. Never refuse their demands. Even if they ask for something difficult, tell them you'll try and later come up with reason how it was not achievable. But don't say 'no' directly.

JUNE 20

"When you're riding, only the race in which you're riding is important." Bill Shoemaker, Jockey

*A trophy you receive after winning a marathon is only
of significance in the marathon department. You cannot
be of eloquent value in the car racing department.*

If you are best at a certain department that doesn't mean that you will know good about the other departments too. You can only master a few arts at a time and focus on that only.

JUNE 21

"A woman of worth is the crown of her husband, but a disgraceful one is like rot in his bones" Proverbs of Solomon (chapter 12-4)

*A virtuous lady is the pride of her husband, whereas
a characterless one is a disgrace to him.*

A woman makes or breaks a home. If your woman is a kind and loyal, she may make your life prosperous and beautiful, and if she is characterless, then your life might be hell.

JUNE 22

"Once you surrender to your vision, success begins to chase you"
The Monk Who Sold His Ferrari

*Once you give up your sleep in the attempt to make your
dream come true, the dream starts unveiling itself unto you.*

I f you have a certain motto to be achieved and you start working
day and night to make it happen, then surely your dream will
ultimately turn into a reality and will no longer remain a dream.

JUNE 23

"The biggest tragedy in America is not the great waste of natural
resources - though this is tragic; the biggest tragedy is the waste of
human resources because the average person goes to his grave with
his music still in him."

— Oliver Wendell Holmes

*The awful tragedy is a wasted talent where a man reaches
his grave without living his dream despite the talent.*

I f you have got certain talent, but you have not utilized, then you're
wasting yourself completely. These skills are God gifted and must
be used wherever necessary to make the most of your talent.

JUNE 24

"Create a definite plan for carrying out your desire and begin at
once, whether you're ready or not, to put this plan into action."

— Napoleon Hill, Motivational Writer

*Never wait till you're ready, execute today – be it
for the sake of dreams, ambitions, and goals.*

I f you are an ambitious person who wants to achieve big in your life, then start working for your goals today. Don't waste time waiting for the right time.

JUNE 25

"I am willing to put myself through anything; temporary pain or discomfort means nothing to me as long as I can see that the experience will take me to a new level."

— Diana Nyad, swimmer

Put aside all your exhaustion and discomfort
if you're willing to step out of the box.

O nce you have decided to achieve something, do not fear about any obstacle and start working on it fearlessly. Step out of your comfort zone and execute it.

JUNE 26

"It is the Lord's blessing that brings wealth, and no effort can substitute it" Proverbs of Solomon

All the exorbitant amount of wealth wouldn't have been
yours solely if God hadn't decided to grant it to you.

E verything a human possesses, whether it be wealth, health or beauty, is a bounty of God to him. So human should not feel proud of all such possessions since it is God who is the owner of it.

JUNE 27

"As long as you're going to be thinking anyway, think big."

— Donald Trump, Real Estate Magnate

You ought to be fantasizing and thinking anyway,
why not to fantasize and think big?

All of us have fantasies. But fantasies shouldn't be about useless stuff. We need to think big, because thinking big will drive you to the big achievements of life.

JUNE 28

"Vision without action is a daydream; action without vision is a nightmare." — Japanese proverb

There is no point of having a vision without
the willingness to put it to practice.

Everyone has dreams and ambitions. But it's all useless to be ambitious if you are not willing to make your dreams come true through hard work and dedication.

JUNE 29

"Accept the challenges so that you may feel the exhilaration of victory."

— George Patton, General

A victory is only worth when you have the battle wounds.

In order to achieve some goal, you must have to go through the process of struggle and hardships. Nothing in this world is free; victory requires battle and its wounds.

JUNE 30

"Don't be afraid to be unique or speak your mind, because that's what makes you different from everyone else."

— Dave Thomas, Wendy's founder

Speak while you have a voice, speak even if your thoughts are different from the rest.

Don't be afraid to be unique or speak your mind, because that's what makes you different from everyone else. And you have got every right to raise your voice.

JULY 1

"Strength does not come from physical capacity. It comes from indomitable will."

— Mahatma Gandhi, statesman

All it takes is a will of steel to achieve things, and physical strength is an absurd phenomenon.

S trong will power will make you go through all the obstacles of life. Being physically strong can't help you in those battles. You can conquer all with strong will power.

JULY 2

"I try to do the right thing at the right time. They may just be little things, but usually they make the difference between winning and losing."

— Kareem Abdul-Jabbar, basketball player

Doing the right thing at the right time – be it too inconsequential or too significant makes a great level of difference in the success or failure of a person.

M ore important than the completion of a certain task is the completion of it at the right time. Time is an important factor when you take on tasks and work upon it. Losing time will take you nowhere.

JULY 3

"A man cannot leave a better legacy to the world than a well-educated family."

— Thomas Scott

The greatest gift that a man can give to his
family is the treasure of education.

E ducation is the asset which you'll possess till the end of your life. Instead of making money for your family's future, provide them good education which will benefit them forever.

JULY 4

"Time is more value than money. You can get more money, but you cannot get more time."

— Jim Rohn, Motivational Speaker

Time never skips a pace and keeps ticking. If
you want to pick its pace, ride along.

Y ou must have heard that 'Time is money.' Well, it's just a myth that time is money because time is way more than that. Never waste your precious time and regret later. Make the most of every minute spent to head towards betterment.

JULY 5

"The world is more malleable than you think, and it's waiting for you to hammer it into shape."

— Bono, musician

The world is like water, and you're much like a container. It
tends to take the shape of you when poured in your container.

W hatever happens in your life you are responsible for it. If you succeed or you fail, it's your actions that have made your place wherever you are in this world.

JULY 6

"In the confrontation between the stream and the rock, the stream always wins, not through strength but by perseverance."

— H. Jackson Brown, Author

Consistency is the key to success. It is the consistent current of the oceans that break rocks despite its rigidity.

I f you have a goal, then be consistent in your behavior to achieve your target. NO matter how much obstacles come in your way to achieve it, your continuous dedication will make you achieve it someday.

JULY 7

"God gives talent, work transforms talent into genius."

—Anna Pavlova

It isn't the talent that makes a man successful but the efforts made in order to accomplish it.

I f you have a talent, but you don't utilize it to gain something, then that talent is totally worthless, but if you put in efforts to utilize that talent than only it's fruitful.

JULY 8

"Education is of no value and talent is worthless - unless you have an unwavering aim. Never find yourself without a compass."

— Condoleezza Rice, Secretary of State

You ought to have a goal and a sense of direction to achieve things in life.

I n order to achieve big, you need to set your goals and then set up a proper plan for the execution of your task. Then only you can accomplish your goals.

JULY 9

"Your ability to discipline yourself "to do what you should, when you should do it, whether you feel like it or not," is the key to becoming a great person and living a great life. When you develop the habits of self-discipline, you will accomplish more in a month than most people accomplish in a year" Bryan Tracy

"Its self-discipline mostly that takes people to different places rather than motivation."

Y ou need to structure yourself before setting up goals. Because in order to execute what you desire, you need to be disciplined and structured to carry out the task each day.

JULY 10

"People do not decide to become extraordinary. They decide to accomplish extraordinary things."

— Sir Edmund Hilary, first to reach the summit of Mount Everest

It's the exceptional things that people aspire to achieve that makes them extraordinary, not their self- drive to be extraordinary.

P eople don't dream out of the blue to become extraordinary. It's their ambitions and well-thought-out measures to achieve the dreams that make them sublime. It's the little strides you take each day that integrate into a bigger and better picture.

JULY 11

"A business is successful to the extent that it provides a product or service that contributes to happiness in all of its forms."

— Mihaly Csikszentmihalyi, Professor of Psychology and Management

*An ideal business is the one through the products
and services of which a customer is happy.*

A happy customer is the company's valuable asset. Therefore, in order to make your business flourish, you need to maintain a good relationship with customers and keep them satisfied through your services.

JULY 12

"Human kindness has never weakened the stamina or softened the fiber of a free people. A nation does not have to be cruel to be tough."

— Franklin Roosevelt, 32nd U.S. president

You can be both kind and tough without having to be cruel to each other. Kindness is the second-best language after love.

K indness is the best act considered after love. You all must be loving and kind to each other, and even if certain things are unacceptable, you can react to them appropriately without getting harsh and cruel.

JULY 13

"Experience is that marvelous thing that enables you to recognize a mistake when you make it again." —F. P. Jones

*The best thing about experience is, it doesn't
let you make the same mistake again.*

T he more experienced you are, the less likely you're to commit mistakes. Experience teaches you a lot about everything.

JULY 14

"Happiness is only a byproduct of successful living."

— Austen Riggs, psychiatrist

When you live a life of your dreams, happiness automatically comes your way.

A lways follow your dreams and do whatever makes you feel happy. If you are living a life following your own dreams, you will automatically be satisfied and happy.

JULY 15

"A leader, once convinced a particular course of action is the right one, must have the determination to stick with it and be undaunted when the going gets rough. "

— Ronald Reagan, 40th U.S. president

Upon realizing one's purpose of life and the mode of action to do that work, one must have the courage to cling to it and carry on regardless of the obstacles.

O nce you have realized what you actually want to do in life and how to do it, you must carry on with it until you get it done completely, no matter how many obstacles come your way.

JULY 16

"The mind is its own place, and in itself can make a heav'n of hell and a hell of a heav'n."

— John Milton, poet

We have both heaven and hell in our minds, what we choose to dominate or recess is what makes us who we are.

E very human being has its own positive and negative traits. But what dominates them is their reality. Never let the evil in you overshadow your good deeds.

JULY 17

"Set goals and objectives, determine priorities, overcome procrastination and gain two extra hours of productive time each day.... successful people get more done and make more money than others by time management" Bryan Tracy

Time management and discipline are what one is supposed to master to achieve their goals.

T ime is money. You need to master the art of time management and make the most out of every minute in order to be successful in life. Wasting time will bring you regrets and failure.

JULY 18

"It comes from saying no to 1,000 things to make sure we don't get on the wrong track or try to do too much. We're always thinking about new markets we could enter, but it's only by saying no that you can concentrate on the things that are really important."

— Steve Jobs, Apple Co-founder

We should learn to say no to others to prioritize things that need to be prioritized.

S et your priorities and focus on them. Don't need to work on anything that's not your interest for the sake of happiness of others. And learn to say no to others.

JULY 19

"I sometimes think that the saving grace of America lies in the fact that the overwhelming majority of Americans are possessed of two great qualities — a sense of humor and a sense of proportion. "

— Franklin Roosevelt, 32nd U.S. president

The fact that America is sustaining today is all accredited to two of their qualities – their great sense of judgment and all the while good humor.

Those civilizations which are attentive to the happenings of their country sustain longer and achieve more in the long run. The citizens of America are known for their grit, shrewdness, knowledge of the surroundings, and a bit of humor, and I think these are what the citizens of every country require to survive.

JULY 20

""Don't tell people how to do things, tell them what to do and let them surprise you with their results. "

— George S. Patton, US Army General

You ought to show people through your actions what needs to be done and be ready to be surprised when they do it your way.

You should be clear about your actions. When dealing with people, you need to be precise and transparent about what you expect and what you want from them, and then they will respond to it accordingly.

JULY 21

"We must become the change we wish to see in the world."

— Mahatma Gandhi, Statesman

*The change we want to see in the world is
the change we ought to practice.*

I f you want this world to be a better place, then you need to be a better person yourself first. Be the change you want!

JULY 22

"The best way to make your dreams come true is to wake up."

— Paul Valery, French Poet

In order to stop dreaming and start executing, you need to wake up.

Y ou need to start working towards the execution of your plans and dreams to make it come true. Otherwise, it will remain a dream forever.

JULY 23

"Influence People and Get What You Want - Using Only Your Words, it's a simple fact - the most successful people in the world are also the best communicators. Your ability to communicate with others will account for fully 85% of your success in your business and in your life" Bryan Tracy

*Effective communication skills can pick a business
from the grounds and take it to heights.*

C ommunication is an important tool to build and maintain a network. If your business has a great team and clients and you know how to communicate and deal with them, then your business will flourish.

JULY 24

"Optimism is essential to achievement and it is also the foundation of courage and true progress."

— Nicholas M. Butler, American Philosopher

*It is required to stay hopeful and practice optimism
at all times in order to achieve milestones.*

Even if you fail once, do not lose hope and keep going. The optimistic approach is the key to success. If you keep on moving forward with this approach, you will achieve your milestone one day.

JULY 25

"Throughout the centuries, there were men who took first steps, down new roads, armed with nothing but their own vision." — Ayn Rand, Novelist

*Back in time, there were men who followed their vision,
took new routes, and discovered new things.*

A person should keep on experimenting. Because such experiments lead to discoveries. If no one ever had a vision and passion for taking new routes and exploring, then this world would have been deprived of so many discoveries.

JULY 26

"It's determination and commitment to an unrelenting pursuit of your goal that will enable you to attain the success you seek."

— Mario Andretti, Race Car Driver

Anything can be achieved through diligence and dedication.

f you have decided to take up challenges in order to achieve something, nothing can stop you. And you will achieve it ultimately.

JULY 27

"Nothing great has ever been achieved except by those who dared believe that something inside them was superior to circumstances."

— Bruce Barton, advertising executive

For those who don't surrender to hurdles,
hurdles surrender to them.

T hose who fear the obstacles and don't move forward will lose, but the one who keeps going without surrendering to hardships will reach his destination for sure.

JULY 28

"When you learn how to Unlock Your Potential you'll know how to Visualize your ideal future and turn it into a reality" Bryan Tracy

You ought to have an idea of capacities and strengths to
maneuver the right plan and make your dream come alive.

f you move in the right direction and execute your plans wisely and properly, then all your goals will be achieved, and you get a chance to live your dreams.

JULY 29

"You miss 100% of the shots you never take." - Wayne Gretzky, Hockey Great

What you never attempt, never get.

Don't hesitate to experiment to attain something in life. You need to make several attempts in order to execute something, but if you don't even try nothing can be done.

JULY 30

Risk-taking is the essential ingredient of success, without the threat of which you can never achieve anything.

Sometimes in order to gain something you need to take risks. Though it has a costly downside, yet its benefits are so pleasing that you shouldn't hesitate to give a chance to it.

JULY 31

"Progress always involves risks. You can't steal second base and keep your foot on first."

— Frederick Wilcox, writer

AUGUST 1

"I just knew, even though I had not yet named the technique, that a gift with a purchase was very appealing."

— Estee Lauder, cosmetics executive

The biggest irony of today is that even the gifts you give others are to be purchased from a gift shop first. Not even the gifts come for free.

The real irony of this era is that even the presents we give to people out of love cost us something when, in fact, it should come for free. It's strange how these gifts have only become an epitome of wealth show off and only gives pleasure to the receiver when it is something really expensive. The world is heading toward worse and becoming more materialistic day by day.

AUGUST 2

"It is through science that we prove, but through intuition that we discover."

—Henri Poincare

We prove through science but discover through intuition.

An idea takes birth in mind, then builds into maneuver when given heed enough and becomes a success when you are determined and curious enough to find the secrets to the universe. It all begins with an idea – an intuition. Therefore, no idea should be taken non-seriously.

AUGUST 3

"A work well begun is half-ended." — Plato, Philosopher

Half of the work is already done when it begins well.

When you give an idea or a maneuver a great and a thoughtful start, most of the work is done then and there. It requires a person to do the homework, lay down the points, make an outline of their tasks, and concentrate on its structure to have most of the concept clear. Once the maneuver is decided, it gets a lot easier to execute the task.

AUGUST 4

"What you lack in talent can be made up with desire, hustle and giving 110% all the time."

— Don Zimmer, Baseball Manager

*The mere act of dreaming reminds us of
what we lack in the first place.*

It's a negative loophole. We as humans tend to dream about things that we don't already have but would love to have. It's either the necessity or the strong desire that springs forth the 'what ifs' of possession. For those who dream are already helpless and in the position of dreaming rather than having. It's where and how the dream begins.

AUGUST 5

"The cave you most fear to enter contains the greatest treasure." —
Joseph Campbell

*The greatest of blessing is concealed behind
the door you are afraid to open.*

I t so happens when you've been struggling for a way so long, you
get tired and stop right when you're about to succeed. This is why
consistency is the best policy to succeed. You work little by little
every day and ultimately reach your goal. The key is not to give
up to the exhaustion because exhaustion itself is a clue that the
milestone is near.

AUGUST 6

"Few men during their lifetime come anywhere near exhausting the
resources dwelling within them. There are deep wells of strength
that are never used."

— Richard Byrd, Explorer

*Few men, during their lifetime, exhaust themselves up
to extract the resources dwelling within them.*

S ome of the men struggle in vain by introspecting and plucking
a purpose that isn't exactly theirs, rather of someone they look
up to. Their lives are imitated, and actions are contradictory. They
waste up their energies in living someone's else dream, which
looked quite like a mirage from afar.

AUGUST 7

"The greatest gift that you can give to others is the gift of unconditional love and acceptance."

— Brian Tracy, Author

Give nothing but love and hope as it is the
best thing to hold out to people.

The mere purpose of human's existence is to spread out the love and utter words of kindness. We as humans are the only hope for each other in times of problems and adversities. It is vital for each human to realize his responsibility toward his fellow beings and other living creatures.

AUGUST 8

"Difficulties in life are intended to make us better not bitter."

— Dan Reeves, Football Coach

"Difficulties in life are intended to make us better, not bitter."

People don't know how necessary adversities are. Mishaps steering sensitivities play well on their part by blinding the individuals into the blues of impossibilities, thus, sweeping the blessings under. Trust me; not all tragedies are meant to shatter you. If you look closely enough, some are wise flukes that intend to make us better rather than bitter.

AUGUST 9

"Make More Friends and Business Contacts...and Be More Attractive to Others! In my travel across the globe, I've had to "charm" my way out of tight situations and win negotiations with difficult people. The Power of Charm saved me more than once and has made a huge impact on my business and personal life—and it will do the same for you! – Bryan Trcay

Charm has been introduced as another tool for business successes.

Charm is a great asset in business dealings. Even the most horrible situations can be settled with negotiation by using charm. It can win the customers, business clients, and even other competitors and bring your company good fortune.

AUGUST 10

"I don't know the key to success, but the key to failure is trying to please everybody. "

— Bill Cosby, Comedian

Living to win the good opinion of others is
too cruel a fate for your success.

The fact that we have a habit of explaining our every possible action account for how much we crave to win the good opinions of others. All those who fear are doomed to live for the satisfaction of others. They care so much about the mundane task of fitting in that they never stand out.

AUGUST 11

"Plans fail when there is no counsel, but they succeed when advisers are many" Proverbs of Solomon (15-22)

*Hear what each employee has to say. Someone
can turn up with a jackpot idea.*

Too many opinions and suggestions can be beneficial for the growth of the company. Every firm has to have a team of advisory and counsel to nudge the company in the right direction. Because out of the many, one opinion can really turn up better for the business.

AUGUST 12

"Asking questions will get you the performance you are after far better than dictating demands."

— Dan James

For those who question are capable of giving the desired results.

The act of questioning begins with an urge to know. The desire for knowledge can open your mind to unfathomable possibilities of life. And this discovery can make you want to learn more. And the more you learn, the more you grow.

AUGUST 13

"All your dreams can come true if you have the courage to pursue them."

— Walt Disney

It takes valor to make a dream come to life.

Everyone is capable of dreaming; only a few can make it come true. It takes real grit, vim, and determination to grab the dream from your vision and pull it into your present.

AUGUST 14

"People die of fright and live of confidence". Henry David, Thoreau, Author, Philosopher

Better to live with confidence than to die each day of fear.

To all those out there who fear and are easily intimidated, this could be the end of you. Fear and intimidation are like slow poisoning before death really takes you. For those who live life with confidence, death trembles to take them away.

AUGUST 15

"If life was so easy that you could just go buy success, there would be a lot more successful companies in the world. Successful enterprises are built from the ground up."

— Lou Gerstner, IBM CEO

Success isn't on sale, or everyone would've been a customer.

If success were on sale, then every organization would've borrowed all the money to get themselves enough successes. But the truth is it isn't. It requires real work of sweat, energy, and determination to achieve your dreams, and it doesn't come overnight either.

AUGUST 16

"What is the true way to wealth? A steady salary can only do so much. Winning the lottery is a pipe dream. There's only one real way to unimaginable wealth, the kind of wealth where you make money hand over fist faster than you can spend it and that way is entrepreneurship" Bryan Tracy

The only way to increase wealth is by investing a handful of it in entrepreneurship.

A wealth that is thoughtfully invested goes a long way and can serve your children. The ideal investment of your money is in entrepreneurship – a business that is solely yours. And then work toward it like a mad man in pursuit of peace. Only this is the key to entrepreneur a successful business.

AUGUST 17

"You have to pretend you're 100% sure. You must take action; you can't hesitate or hedge your bets. Anything less will condemn your efforts to failure. "

— Andrew Grove, Intel co-founder

Anything you do, do it with confidence and certainty. Even a little doubt invites failure.

K nowledge is the confidence that you wear on your face, and everyone comes attracted to you. That's the thing about confidence and conviction; it makes others believe all of what you say. In everything you do, let confidence be the main and never allow doubt to cross your face or mind as it only invites failure.

AUGUST 18

"In prosperity our friends know us; in adversity, we know our friends."

— John Churton Collins

*There are times when you shine; you find everyone
standing in line. Then there comes a time when you
aren't fine; you find none in your decline.*

People are more attracted to glory and self-sufficient ones that they tend to buzz around them like busy bees. Everyone wants to be surrounded by educated and highly esteemed people and want to win their friendship and good opinion. But when that person's rank falls in society due to a financial downfall, these busy bees disappear as quickly as they came. Such is the nature of men with the exception of rare few who understands that everyone undergoes such phases in life.

AUGUST 19

"The key to successful time management is doing the most important task first, and giving it your full concentration, to the exclusion of everything else."

— Alex MacKenzie

*The rule of time management is to set out to
perform the very first task on the list.*

What a man of discipline is supposed to do is to plan out the structure if he doesn't want to run out of time in the face of the tight deadlines. The easiest way to manage time is by listing down your tasks, top to bottom, priority wise, and then rule out the first one after working on it. It tends to keep your focus straight without distractions.

AUGUST 20

"Obstacles cannot crush me. Every obstacle yields to stern resolve."

— Leonardo da Vinci, Artist

*No hurdles can do me wrong because they were
the very first to teach me persistence.*

W hen you undergo so many adversities in life, you tend to take each storm as a challenge. You take each brick thrown by life your way and start building a house, and that's the greatest gift that tribulation can give you. And there comes a time you start enjoying the challenges that life sends your way.

AUGUST 21

"I've learned that people will forget what you said, people will forget what you did, but people will never forget how you made them feel."

— Maya Angelou, Poet

*All your kind actions would be to no avail if
you made a person feel pathetic.*

W ords are merely words hanging loosely on the tip of your tongue requiring nothing but a little jerk to utter promises and commitment. The other person only tends to watch for your action because words are easy to deliver. But the good news is even the actions lose its significance when your attitude breaks in. If you made a person feel worthless, upset or pathetic, chances are they'll never forget it. So, it all gets down to how you treat them and make them feel.

AUGUST 22

"Increase Your Contacts, Expand Your Influence and Build Your Business...FAST! You've heard the saying... "it's not WHAT you know, but WHO you know"... how many times has this proved to be true?" Bryan Tracy

The bigger your network, the greater your influence and value.

Different experience and expertise come from knowing different people and their diverse mindsets. It makes you a people's person, grow your networks, increases your influence and exposure, which only helps you later. You come immediately in the mind of people when an opportunity comes, or they seek out a competent individual to look up to. Also, if you are stuck up and seek out help, you tend to know whom to approach and ask for help in your big circle. A big network is always a win-win situation for an individual.

AUGUST 23

"It's the little things that make the big things possible. Only close attention to the fine details of any operation makes the operation first class."

— J. Willard Marriot

Don't get fooled by the appeal of little things for they aren't as little as they appear to be.

No matter what you're working toward, all that is required to make it excellent is the attention to little details. When these little pointers are worked on effectively, the entire work turns up to be perfect.

AUGUST 24

A good marriage is when you're married not to someone you can live with, but to someone you really cannot live without."

— Dr. Howard Hendricks

*Marry the one who values you rather than
one who needs you to satisfy himself.*

A person in love is in the position to be addicted to you. Choose your partner wisely. It is always important to pick someone who is willing to overlook all your flaws, bad habits, and scars and accept you for who you are. Marry the one who values *what and who you are* and still can't go a single day without you rather than someone who needs you but for a while.

AUGUST 25

"Choice, not chance, determines human destiny."

— Robert W. Ellis

It's the quality of choices we make that decides our future.

Little by little, we stride toward success, little by little we can make just enough out of our every day and little by little we get sick each day till we ultimately die. It's the little things that turn up to be bigger. Hence, we have to be vigilant with the little decisions we make every day as they play a significant role in making or running our future.

AUGUST 26

"If you don't drive your business, you will be driven out of business."
— B. C. Forbes, Founder of Forbes Magazine

If you don't act out your plan today, you'll have to work for others.

R ationality is in starting up a business of your own. Break your sweat and rust into achieving what is actually your passion rather than working for others where you are treated like a servant who is hired to fulfill and work on their dreams. If you don't start up your business today, you have no job security in the business of others. You wouldn't want to be in someone else's business with no self-respect.

AUGUST 27

"The wise are more powerful than the strong, and the learned than the mighty, for by strategy war is waged, and victory depends on many counselors" Proverbs of Solomon (24-5,6)

It takes wise to defeat an army.

T he wise is a superpower and stronger than physical strength. A learned man reigns over an illiterate king who seeks who his help and advice from time to time. The wise know the right way to maneuver actions, and the illiterate king counts on him to devise a strategy for the war. The victory doesn't come without the involvement of too many active bodies and racking brains employed in the process.

AUGUST 28

""We make a living by what we get. We make a life by what we give."

— Winston Churchill, British prime minister

You only get what you deserve and give
what others deserve to receive.

G od, as the master planner, governing each of our lives, only gives us what is meant for us. The rest is unto us to make a good living out of what is given to us. For those of us who are granted more by His generosity, have a noblesse oblige to give out more often to the underprivileged.

AUGUST 29

"As a coach, your high standards of performance, attention to detail and-above all-how hard you work set the stage for how your players perform."

— Don Shula, Football Coach

A right coach is attentive to all the details.

A coach has to have a know-how of the potential and stamina of each individual in the team. He should have good analytical skills and stay quite attentive to the little details – be it the hours or type of training required to taste the victory. In addition, he also knows when to snap and when to retreat.

AUGUST 30

"The man who chases two rabbits catches neither."

— Confucius, philosopher

When you set out to perform two tasks at
a time, neither of them is done.

W hile planning out how to perform a task, it's always important to keep your eyes fixed on the target that is required to be achieved. The distractions have a way of hindering your sight, but the absolute resolve and focus are what that determine the duration of the task completion. Don't start doing two things at a time, as it confuses you and makes you incapable of completing either of the tasks.

AUGUST 31

"The fact is, everyone is in sales. Whatever area you work in, you do have clients and you do need to sell."

— Jay Abraham, Marketing Expert

In this era of saturated markets and multiple products, everyone is busy selling.

I n today's era, so many businesses have emerged out of nowhere and taken over the market by storm. Every organization is busy selling themselves in the shape of their products and services. In between, the customers are occupied with lots of options to go for while the sellers impose the good image – false or not, of their products and services on others.

SEPTEMBER 1

"An organization's ability to learn, and translate that learning into action rapidly, is the ultimate competitive business advantage."

— Jack Welch, General Electric CEO

A business has to have good adaptation and learning skills to immediately implement new ideas and gain a competitive edge.

I f you have a good base and clear concepts because of your strong foundation, then you are capable of giving good and realistic ideas and secure a better place in the business market.

SEPTEMBER 2

"Every great dream begins with a dreamer. Always remember, you have within you the strength, the patience and the passion to reach for the stars to change the world."

— Harriet Tubman, Abolitionist

Every successful person once started with a dream, and then his persistence, strength, and passion came to play to make it come true.

Y ou have to take the first stride up to climb the stairs, and this first stride is a step up the mountain. Allow your pursuit and passion never to stop you from chasing it and eventually, because of that constant try; you will achieve it.

SEPTEMBER 3

"Let others lead small lives, but not you. Let others argue over small things, but not you. Let others cry over small hurts, but not you. Let others leave their future in someone else's hands, but not you."

—Jim Rohn

Don't envy and follow the crowd. Have your own way of doing things. Most of the ways adopted by them aren't correct anyway.

Don't look what others have and a desire to have it as well. Everyone in this world gives certain things which cannot be owned by everybody because maybe that certain thing isn't made for you or maybe there is something better you have, or maybe the thing they have isn't worth to be desired for.

SEPTEMBER 4

""You can never cross the ocean unless you have the courage to lose sight of the shore." —Christopher Columbus

Keep your eyes fixated to the moon; the entire loop of darkness is blinding.

Always look on the bright side of the story, the goods which will be helping you to give something positive in life and don't let your dark side take over you.

SEPTEMBER 5

"When one door of happiness closes, another opens; but often we look so long at the closed door that we do not see the one that has opened for us." —Helen Keller

At times the agony of the missed opportunity blinds us from seeing the new opportunity opened to us.

The regrets of missing out the good opportunity sometimes don't let us look at the other opportunities that we have on our ways which might turn out to be good for our future.

SEPTEMBER 6

"We are what we imagine. Our very existence consists in our imagination of ourselves. The greatest tragedy that can befall us is to go unimagined." —N. Scott Momaday

What we assume ourselves to be is what we turn up to be in front of others. So long as we imagine ourselves, we are circulating what we assume to get across.

If we think of ourselves as a nice and good person, then others will think the same about us. What we think is what we become.

SEPTEMBER 7

"Destiny is not a matter of chance, it is a matter of choice. It is not a thing to be waited for, it is a thing to be achieved." —William Jennings Bryan

We harvest what we sow.

We make our destiny for ourselves. It doesn't bump into us by chance. Whatever we do to others, good or bad, it returns back to us in times of need and despair.

SEPTEMBER 8

"There is no chance, no destiny, no fate that can circumvent or hinder or control the firm resolve of a determined soul." —Ella Wheeler Wilcox

No setbacks can get in the way of a person resolved to succeed.

If a person is out and about on his new venture related to his purpose, then nothing can stop him or come in his way.

SEPTEMBER 9

"Life is not discovery of fate; it is continuous creation of future, through choices of thoughts, feelings and actions in the present."
—Sanjay Sahay

Our future is composed of the little choices, decisions, and actions we execute one day at a time.

O ur future is based on what we are doing in our present life. The small moments, decisions, and choice that we make today forecast what is going to happen in our future.

SEPTEMBER 10

"You were born an original. Don't die a copy." —John Mason

You are your original version. Don't waste your example by imitating others and their passion.

E very person is unique. None is the same in this world. We are imperfect. Don't envy and follow others. You have your own beautiful self which s gifted to you by God.

SEPTEMBER 11

"The pen that writes your life story must be held in your own hand." —Irene C. Kassorla

Be the author, and every once in a while, the editor of your story. Don't let others write for you.

D on't let the others make decisions of your life and tell you what step to take. Live your life and see the path you are walking on. If obstacles come, don't change the route, face it like a pro. Learn from your mistake.

SEPTEMBER 12

"Out of clutter, find simplicity. From discord, find harmony. In the middle of difficulty lies opportunity." —Albert Einstein

Nothing in life comes to destruct you but to teach you lessons and learn from it so that you can walk carefully.

E xtract a little sunshine from the ruthless winter, borrow a little joy from the occasional despair and pick a little strength from the setbacks. And in the middle of adversity, you'll find a ray of hope.

SEPTEMBER 13

"Nothing truly valuable arises from ambition or from a mere sense of duty; it stems rather from love and devotion towards men and towards objective things." —Albert Einstein

All of what a man aims for has to be collectively for the betterment of society.

W henever a person set his goal, he should make it sure that it doesn't affect the society in a negative way but should be for the good cause of it.

SEPTEMBER 14

"To serve is beautiful, but only if it is done with joy and a whole heart." —Pearl S. Buck

Any act of kindness goes in vain if it isn't done from the whole heart.

A deed which is done with a pure intention and a good heart can never be wasted because it is something which is done selflessly and out of love.

SEPTEMBER 15

"How do we keep our inner fire alive? Two things, at minimum, are needed: an ability to appreciate the positives in our life - and a commitment to action." —Nathaniel Branden

There are two ways to keep our spark alive: to
stay optimistic and committed to action.

One can never lose hope of living a good life if whatever he does it is with his fully honest commitments without expecting anything in return and while staying positive and thinking on the bright side as being optimistic.

SEPTEMBER 16

"Let him who would enjoy a good future waste none of his present." —Roger Babson

He who is gifted shall use his talent and not waste his time.

If a person knows he has a talent, then he shouldn't waste it and keep practicing it for his own sake and sanity.

SEPTEMBER 17

"It takes great courage to faithfully follow what we know to be true." —Sara E. Anderson

Mark of a courageous person is he does what he believes
to be true regardless of the opinion of others.

Every person is out there in this world to give opinions, sometimes those opinions are correct but sometimes when they aren't everyone gets affected. If a person is confident about his own opinion, then he must not listen to others and try to follow what he believes rather than disturbing his perspective.

SEPTEMBER 18

"Our background and circumstances may have influenced who we are, but we are responsible for who we become." —Barbara Geraci

Irrespective of the background and families we come from, what we struggle to become still plays a significant role in making us who we are.

S ometimes the things that define us are the struggles that we go through to reach a certain height in our life rather than from where we come from and who our ancestors were.

SEPTEMBER 19

"Great thoughts speak only to the thoughtful mind, but great actions speak to all Mankind." —Emily P. Bissell — Cesar Ritz, hotelier

Unique thoughts may entertain the thoughtful mind, but good execution sets an example among mankind.

T here are many thinkers among us, but only a few have the potential to turn their thoughts into reality. It is vital for a person to work so hard that his reality starts extracts the desired action from his dream.

SEPTEMBER 20

"We all live under the same sky, but we don't all have the same horizon." —Konrad Adenauer

We all are the same yet different. Two different people can see the sunset in an entirely different manner.

E veryone is different, and so are their perspectives on everything. As separate individuals, we deal with the same thing in different manners and look at it quite differently than others.

SEPTEMBER 21

"Time is the coin of your life. It is the only coin you have, and only you can determine how it will be spent. Be careful lest you let other people spend it for you." —Carl Sandburg

What's common between time and money is that
you have good control over spending it. And they
both demand to be spent thoughtfully.

Money and time are two different things which have to be spent wisely. You need to have a good understanding of how to spend them, in a manner that it serves for the greater good of mankind and doesn't go in vain.

SEPTEMBER 22

"The best career advice to give the young is, find out what you like doing best and get someone else to pay you for doing it." — Katherine Whilehaen

One must never do what he's best at free of cost.

If a person has a skill and he is aware that he is really good at it, then he must not waste this gift by employing it for free as it is an opportunity to avail for the cost of your skill and talent.

SEPTEMBER 23

"The gem cannot be polished without friction nor man without trials." —Confucius

The way gems need to be rubbed to get the shine, in the same
way, a man needs to face hurdles to grow and stand out.

Failure is that element of life through which a person learns to grow. A person who has never faced any difficulty in life cannot rise up and walk again. During the fall, he is required to stand back up, learn the reason for his fall and should try not to repeat the mistake ever again.

SEPTEMBER 24

"Hands that serve are holier than lips that pray." —Sai Baba

It's always generous actions that matter more than kind words.

Actions speak louder than words. Whenever we are in a difficult phase of our life, we always want someone to be there for us. It is during difficulty we need someone to stand there with us, help us with little healings rather than just giving us false hopes of their availability. It's always actions that soothe the aching soul.

SEPTEMBER 25

"To be yourself in a world that is constantly trying to make you something else is the greatest accomplishment." —Ralph Waldo Emerson

Greatest is the man who doesn't pick tempting influences quickly.

A person who doesn't get carried away is wiser as he doesn't go with the flow and don't follow what the world is running after.

SEPTEMBER 26

"Feeling gratitude and not expressing it is like wrapping a present and not giving it."

— William Arthur Ward, Scholar

Gratitude is meant to be expressed for the
person to know how it made you feel.

You need to show gratitude to the person who made you feel loved and valuable. He should be acknowledged about his contribution to making you feel good and how you are overwhelmed by their generosity.

SEPTEMBER 27

"I think the purpose of life is to be useful, to be responsible, to be honorable, to be compassionate. It is, after all, to matter: to count, to stand for something, to have made some difference that you lived at all." —Leo C. Rosten

While you live, make the most of each moment.
You owe the earth what you are gifted with, so find
your purpose and be useful to your planet.

Get across the skills that you have been gifted with. This planet is your home, and it has the right to witness all the goodness residing in here as we owe it for space and food it is providing us.

SEPTEMBER 28

When a mind of man can conceive, and believe, it can achieve. Thoughts are things. And powerful things at that, when mixed with definiteness of purpose, and burning desire, can be translated into riches." Napoleon Hill

What you believe is what you achieve. Success is mostly
the result of irresistible urge and defined vision.

Focusing on a certain set of goals can give the direction of what to strive for and achieve. If you are optimistic about achieving them, then at the end of the day the victory is yours. Remember, pure intentions and firm-believe is the key.

SEPTEMBER 29

"Feeling gratitude and not expressing it is like wrapping a present and not giving it."

— William Arthur Ward, Scholar

We ought to give the present of gratitude to the ones who never left us in times of need. Gratitude deserves to.

We owe the person who has never left our side in times of need and tribulation. Our mouth should only utter words of gratitude for them as they are worth it. Gratitude can be depicted through our demeanor and mouth as these are the two exits it has.

SEPTEMBER 30

The winners in life think constantly in terms of I can, I will, and I am. Losers, on the other hand, concentrate their waking thoughts on what they should have done, or what they can't do." Dennis Waitley

What differentiates a winner from a loser is that one is quite confident in what he does, while the other is full of regrets over the past mistakes and suspicious about everything.

If a person dwells on the past, regretting his mistakes or confused about the choices to make in the present, then he can never be successful. It takes real confidence to face the world with a dream by your side and grin at all the raising brows.

OCTOBER 1

"Toil and risk are the price of glory, but it is a lovely thing to live with courage and die leaving an everlasting fame." —Alexander the Great

You ought to risk some of your fortunes to watch your business flourishing. In the end, all of it makes sense when you leave a legacy of your success behind.

W hen you start a business and struggle to flourish it, you will face a lot of troubles, and you might lose a lot to reach your target. But by the end of the day you will be successful and when you by chance will look behind you won't regret the loss but cherish your journey and your present even more.

OCTOBER 2

"The important thing is not being afraid to take a chance. Remember, the greatest failure is to not try. Once you find something you love to do, be the best at doing it". Debbi Fields

It's better to try and give your best in the making of something than to have regret over unused skills and unspent energy.

Y ou should not hesitate to start with something new owing to the fear of failure. Because later, even if you fail, you will not have many regrets as you tried your best and gave it your all. You should utilize the skills in you and don't let them go to waste.

OCTOBER 3

"It is our choices that show what we truly are, far more than our abilities." —J.K. Rowling

It's the decisions we make, regardless of our potential, that reflects our true self.

We should always move out of our comfort zone and make a decision based on what is beneficial to us. Our decisions should reflect our desires and dreams.

OCTOBER 4

"To give real service you must add something which cannot be bought or measured with money, and that is sincerity and integrity."
—Donald A. Adams

To all the businesses out there who want to make many customers
must sell what money cannot buy i-e integrity and honesty.

In dealing with your customers, the key factor to bind them is transparency and honesty. All businesses must be sincere to the customers because a happy customer is a business's valuable asset.

OCTOBER 5

"When you are inspired by some great purpose, some extraordinary project, all your thoughts break their bonds: Your mind transcends limitations, your consciousness expands in every direction, and you find yourself in a new, great, and wonderful world. Dormant forces, faculties and talents become alive, and you discover yourself to be a greater person by far than you ever dreamed yourself to be."
—Patanjali

Make big goals and invest all in it you will end
up as an erudite person than yesterday.

When you aspire to achieve a big goal, you employ all your thoughts, sincerity, dedication, and actions into making that one dream come true. And in the end, when you finally achieve it, you find yourself as a better and more erudite person than yesterday.

OCTOBER 6

"You will recognize your own path when you come upon it, because you will suddenly have all the energy and imagination you will ever need." —Jerry Gillies

Listen to what your heart says; then follow it.

First, you need to identify a purpose hidden deep within your heart. And when you find it, then everything starts making sense. It is during this moment you are required to erupt with all the energy and determination to make a grab for it.

OCTOBER 7

"When you see what you're here for, the world begins to mirror your purpose in a magical way. It's almost as if you suddenly find yourself on a stage in a play that was written expressly for you." — Betty Sue Flowers

Identify the purpose of your life; you will conquer the world.

When you find your real purpose in life, all the puzzling pieces start to join before your eyes and make a perfect picture that you couldn't fathom earlier. And you feel as if this world is for you to conquer.

OCTOBER 8

"Your time is limited, so don't waste it living someone else's life and don't let the noise of others' opinions drown out your own inner voice. Most important, have the courage to follow your heart and intuition. They somehow already know what you truly want to become." —Steve Jobs

That inner voice is going to take you places.

T ime is fleeting, and so is your stay on earth. It's hard to maintain your inner voice amidst the frantic noise of the crowd, but it is unto us not let that little voice mix up with the roar of the crowd. That inner voice is going to take you places.

OCTOBER 9

"True happiness is not attained through self-gratification, but through fidelity to a worthy purpose." –Helen Keller

The time spent in laboring your purpose is a time well spent.

Y ou should identify the purpose of your life and then spend the rest of your life to fulfill that purpose. And the time spent on your purpose will ultimately be worth it.

OCTOBER 10

"People who consider themselves victims of their circumstances will always remain victims unless they develop a greater vision for their lives." —Stedman Graham

You never recover from a tragedy unless you're willing to heal.

F or those who seek the sympathy of others tend to portray themselves as a victim. While some may actually be needing help, a kind word or a comforting gesture but none of it is to any avail. Since the more attention we need due to our tragedy, the more we are reminded of the wrong done to us. And in this way, we never heal. It is better to take notes from what we have undergone and welcome the new sun every day.

OCTOBER 11

"Too many of us are not living our dreams because we are living our fears." —Les Brown

Fears are the killer of dreams. And sadly, some of us allow these fears to swallow our dreams and never step out to make big changes in the world.

You should not let fear hinder your way from achieving big. But sadly, some of us allow these fears to swallow our dreams and never step out to make big changes in the world.

OCTOBER 12

"I want to sing like the birds sing, not worrying about who hears or what they think." — Rumi

We should let go of our fear of being misjudged and do what we please.

Don't let other's opinion shatter your dreams. People hesitate to experiment out of fear of judgment. We should not bother about other's opinion because they matter the least.

OCTOBER 13

"Love without action is meaningless and action without love is irrelevant." —Deepak Chopra

You ought to express your love through actions. Without the little acts of showing love, your love story can never prosper.

Learn to express your feelings. Without the little acts of showing love and respect, your love story can never prosper.

OCTOBER 14

"To understand the heart and mind of a person, look not at what he has already achieved, but at what he aspires to do." —Kahlil Gibran

*The achievements of a person don't define him
as much as his goals and aspirations.*

A person's goals and aspirations are more a matter of concern than his achievements in life for the sake of being called 'a big man.' No matter how successful you become, never forget your values.

OCTOBER 15

"When you were born, you cried and the world rejoiced. Live your life so that when you die, the world cries and you rejoice." — Cherokee Expression

OCTOBER 16

"Truly loving another means letting go of all expectations. It means full acceptance, even celebration of another's personhood." — Karen Casey

*A person comes into this world crying but should
amaze death by leaving with a smile.*

This world is a temporary place. Make this experience a worthy one and exit this place satisfied without any regret. After all, not all of us have much longer here.

OCTOBER 17

"It is not how much we do, but how much love we put in the doing. It is not how much we give, but how much love we put in the giving." —Mother Teresa

> *Whatever you do, do it with love. Whatever you*
> *give, give it with the purest intention.*

L ove is a feeling of passion; whenever we love something, we want to invest in it with a good intention and pure heart. We give our energy selflessly. Similarly, love whatever task you are given and then see you will enjoy doing it and the output will be really good too.

OCTOBER 18

"We look forward to the time when the Power of Love will replace the Love of Power. Then will our world know the blessings of Peace." –William E. Gladstone

> *I dream of a world where the power of love reigns over the*
> *love of power and the world will then live in peace forever.*

L ove and power are two different forces. Power can become destructive at a point if used as a negative element, while love cannot be misused. The world is a place with both forces balancing it, but if the power is canceled with love, then this world can become a place of long-lasting peace.

OCTOBER 19

"We don't stop playing because we grow old; we grow old because we stop playing." – George Bernard Shaw

We grow old the day we outgrow toys, not the day
we began to feel old. It's important to have a child-
like state of wonder at every stage of life.

J oy and goals are very necessary for our lives as they don't make
you feel old. We all should have goals and small moments of joy
to keep us alive.

OCTOBER 20

"I've come to believe that each of us has a personal calling that's
as unique as a fingerprint - and that the best way to succeed is to
discover what you love and then find a way to offer it to others in
the form of service, working hard, and allowing the energy of the
universe to lead you." –Oprah Winfrey

The talent of a person is as distinctive as his facial features.
It is required for a person to discover his passion, gear up to
achieve it, and then propose it to others for their learning.

E veryone in this world is gifted with talent. Some of us struggle
to know if we have discovered the gift or not. Once we know it,
we are supposed to work on it with passion and then tell the world
about it with confidence.

OCTOBER 21

"The purpose of life is not to fight against evil and misfortune; it is
to unveil magnificence." –Alan Cohen

The world only reveals its secret when we conspire to look for
it rather than setting out to eradicate the evil from the world.

E verything has its own good, if we try to find and focus on the
good side rather than criticizing everything, then layer by layer

the roots of good sides will start to open up on us, and something very rare and precious will be revealed to us.

OCTOBER 22

"A ship in harbor is safe, but that is not what ships are for." –John A. Shedd

A bird is safe in a cage, but that's not
what its wings are designed for.

Humans are made to learn and explore, if a child isn't allowed to go out and make friends for fear of bad influence, then at one point in life when he will face a bad situation and wouldn't know what to do due to the lack of experience. You have to fail time and again to learn and explore the world.

OCTOBER 23

"Your vision will become clear only when you can look into your own heart. Who looks outside, dreams, who looks inside awakes." —Carl Gustav Jung October 24

The key to finding your vision is to dig deep inside your
soul and ask where does your mind wander when it's free.
The answer to this question is the purpose of your life.

If you are confused and don't know what is the purpose of your life, then you really need to ask yourself questions. Talk to yourselves, ask what is your passion, what you love, what you want to give, which world you want to be live in, and the answer to that question is the purpose of your living.

OCTOBER 24

"Wisdom is knowing what path to take next... Integrity is taking it." "We can't change the wind, but we can adjust the sails." "If you don't design your own life plan, chances are you'll fall into someone else's plan. And guess what they have planned for you? Not much." —Jim Rohn

If you don't plan for yourself, then others plan for you.

For instance, you are often stuck up working for an organization struggling to meet their organizational goals rather than yours. You ought to introspect and retrospect your aims and ambitions to hire others rather than be hired.

OCTOBER 25

"The meaning of life is to give life meaning." —Ken Hudgins

The purpose of life is to find the purpose of life
in a manner that does others good.

Doing good to others is the righteous deed. Everyone's purpose in life should be to find a way to make others life joyful and happy.

OCTOBER 26

"Though no one can go back and make a brand-new start, anyone can start from now and make a brand-new ending." —Carl Bard

Even though the beginning was not in our control,
the ending still is. To begin working on our
purpose today can make our ending well.

The past cannot be changed, but the future is in our hand, either we can make it good and easy for us by working on our present or make it difficult by dwelling in the past.

OCTOBER 27

"It's never too late to be what you might have been." —George Elliot

It's never to later to chase your dreams. Age is just a
number when your will and persistence is strong.

Never restrict yourself to achieve a goal that you have set for yourself or a dream that you still are wishing on to come true because of your age. It's isn't the age that defines what is achievable and what isn't. Keeping going after your goals and dreams.

OCTOBER 28

"Life's like a movie; write your own ending, keep believing, keep pretending..." —Jim Henson

Write your story for yourself or else others will write for you.
The beginning may not be good but make the ending worth.

Never let the others make the decisions for you. Your life is yours. Start planning for it. Perhaps, many things won't work out, or they might be difficult for you, but the end will be beautiful.

OCTOBER 29

"Twenty years from now you will be more disappointed by the things that you didn't do than by the ones you did do. So throw off the bowlines. Sail away from the safe harbor. Catch the trade winds in your sails. Explore. Dream. Discover." —Mark Twain

Dream, maneuver and execute today to escape the regrets later.

Start working on your goals today, and try to fix your present, so you don't have time for regrets in the future.

OCTOBER 30

"The greatest danger for most of us is not that our aim is too high and we miss it, but that it is too low and we reach it."
—Michelangelo

The problem isn't in aiming big but in aiming convenient.

S et big goals, so that you can work hard to achieve your goals. And never set limitation to your dreams which will make you lazy to achieve them.

OCTOBER 31

"Strange is our situation here upon earth. Each of us comes for a short visit, not knowing why, yet sometimes seeming to divine a purpose. From the standpoint of daily life, however, there is one thing we do know - that man is here for the sake of other men." — Albert Einstein

The other purposes of existence must be vague to mankind, but the one that comes clean is we are here to each other.

T he other person's purpose in our lives is a secret to us; we don't know what lesson are they holding for us in-store, but we should know that we have them if we need a shoulder to cry on or someone to talk to.

NOVEMBER 1

"Man is not a being who stands still, he is a being in the process of becoming. The more he enables himself to become, the more he fulfills his true mission." —Rudolph Steiner

All the rigidity is in our minds. Man is, in fact, forever malleable and in the process of learning.

A man's mind is like a computer with matchless storage capacity and energy. He is naturally bestowed with the greatest of potential and capacity to expand their brains and accept as much information as possible. So, the people who make their minds rigid are the stubborn ones who strongly abide by a belief system. When, in fact, the learning phase of a human never ends.

NOVEMBER 2

"The person without a purpose is like a ship without a rudder." — Thomas Carlyle

A man without a vision is like a sky without the sun – dark and blinding.

Without a vision, there is no sense of direction. Without the direction, there is no destination. And living without a destination is a purposeless life with no happy moments.

NOVEMBER 3

"A man is ethical only when life, as such, is sacred to him, that of plants and animals as that of his fellow men, and when he devotes himself helpfully to all life that is in need of help." —George Orwell

The real ethics of a man is reflected in his gesture of kindness toward his fellow beings and animals.

The virtue of a man is reflected in his actions. The way a man treats his fellow beings tells you a lot about his upbringing. A man of virtue is not the only kind to his fellow humans but also animals and anything that is alive.

NOVEMBER 4

"Life isn't about finding yourself. Life is about creating yourself."
—George Bernard Shaw

Most of the men have achieved more by making themselves what they were not instead of digging themselves to extract a vision.

The greatest transformation ever witnessed by mankind is of a man who has changed himself entirely to attain a goal beneficial for humanity than investing his time on finding his real purpose to work on. After all, the real purpose of men is to serve his fellow men.

NOVEMBER 5

"He who dares nothing need hope for nothing." "Far better is it to dare mighty things, to win glorious triumphs - even though checkered by failure - than to rank with those poor spirits who neither enjoy much nor suffer much, because they live in a gray twilight that knows not victory nor defeat." — Theodore Roosevelt

Step out of your shell before it swallows every spark of you.

He, who dares not step out of his comfort zone, never travels places or accomplishes riches. Then there comes a time when he becomes too numb to both joy and sorrow.

NOVEMBER 6

"You will recognize your own path when you come upon it, because you will suddenly have all the energy and imagination you will ever need." —Jerry Gillies

The universe is quite helpful once you
find what you are made to do.

When a person finds his purpose, the universe automatically builds all the energy and zeal it could to make that person achieve it.

NOVEMBER 7

"When you see what you're here for, the world begins to mirror your purpose in a magical way. It's almost as if you suddenly find yourself on a stage in a play that was written expressly for you." — Betty Sue Flowers

That's the thing about passion; it can be
seen by others in your eyes.

When your vision flashes before your eyes, the world starts to encourage you as to how achievable is your goal and how you should go for it.

NOVEMBER 8

"True happiness is not attained through self-gratification, but through fidelity to a worthy purpose." –Helen Keller

The sweat you break springs forth the feeling of accomplishment.

When you invest all of yourself – be it energy, power, wealth, and skillset, into achieving what you aim for, that's where real happiness begins to enter your life.

NOVEMBER 9

"It's never too late to change the programming imprinted in childhood, carried in our genes or derived from previous lives; the solution is mindfulness in the present moment." —Peter Shepherd

You may be conditioned to behave in a certain way, but then again, every habit is pretty much malleable by the living utmost in the present.

For people raised in ugly settings do bear the germs or trauma of that setting, but pretty everything is recoverable when you don't dwell in the past and start living in the present.

NOVEMBER 10

"Love is patient, love is kind. It does not envy, it does not boast, it is not proud. It is not rude, it is not self-seeking, it is not easily angered, it keeps no record of wrongs. Love does not delight in evil but rejoices with the truth. It always protects, always trusts, always hopes, always perseveres... And now these three remain: faith hope and love. But the greatest of these is love." —Bible (I Corinthians 13:4-7, 13)

Love is a glimpse of heaven on earth.

He, who has no wealth, but love, can survive easily on love alone. As it provides with all the tenderness, warmth, and courage to rise above all the worries, hardships, and storms.

NOVEMBER 11

"Only through love can we obtain communion with God." —Albert Schweitzer

God is fluent in love.

There is one language known to God, and that is love. He rises us through warmth and compassion in the face of difficulty and gives us courage in the face of doubt.

NOVEMBER 12

"In the place of stillness, rises potential. From the place of potential, emerges possibility. Where there is possibility, there is choice. And where there is choice, there is freedom!" —Gabrielle Goddard

When you aren't looking for something, it emerges out of the blue and takes you to different heights.

When there is a calmness for a long time, chances are seed is going to sprout from that area. The potential of a person generates from a place where there is stillness. It is from the same place where potential erupts from, comes a number of possibilities. And possibilities breed forth healthy choices, and these choices constitute our life.

NOVEMBER 13

"All major religious traditions carry basically the same message, that is love, compassion and forgiveness ... the important thing is they should be part of our daily lives." —Dalai Lama

All the religions impart the same message of love, humanity, and righteous acts.

There is one thing common in all religion; there all are in support of the virtuous behavior of men. The point of religion is to save us from the evils of existence and guide us to the right path.

NOVEMBER 14

"You yourself, as much as anybody in the entire universe, deserve your love and affection." —Buddha

Everyone in this world deserves a fair amount of love, care, and compassion to make it through every day.

E very soul on this planet is thirsty of love, care, and compassion. Without it, a person is completely hopeless and incapable of performing regular tasks. No matter how stern, rational, and professional a person may seem, there still comes a time when he craves a gentle touch, warmth and a goodnight kiss. Factors which alone are enough for a person to have a bright morning the next day.

NOVEMBER 15

"Forgiveness is the attribute of the strong." —Mahatma Gandhi

The weak can never forgive.

T he act of forgiveness comes out of generosity. It springs forth from the understanding that human is to err, and mistakes are the inevitable part of life. It comes from the realization that you too can be in the helpless and repenting position of seeking someone's forgiveness because of your blunders. It isn't the trait of the weak, who is void of any empathy and understanding of human's mistakes. Only the strong can forgive.

NOVEMBER 16

"It is not the answer that enlightens, but the question." —Decouvertes

The answers to questions asked out of curiosity can stay in your mind forever.

That is the great thing about the question that in the asking itself is a realization that you are capable of finding reasons relevant to the working mechanism. The mere act of questioning comes from a deep interest concerning the context and learning exactly begins from there. And the satisfactory answers to these questions itself stay in mind forever, if not, the person himself sets out to find it, and that alone is the purpose of education.

NOVEMBER 17

"Choose being kind over being right, and you'll be right every time." —Richard Carlson

In this era, there is an evolving need of being
kind more often than being right.

There is no right and wrong way of doing things. It's just overly employed and not-so-frequently -employed ways of doing things. The most frequently employed way became a norm and considered the right way. What may be right for you couldn't always be right for everyone else. Only kindness and empathy are the right acts regardless of who it is showered on.

NOVEMBER 18

"Insight occurs when, and to the degree that, one knows oneself." —Andrew Schneider

Insight comes with the realization of who you are.

There comes a point in everyone's life when he is introduced to himself. Some call it epiphany and some coin it -insight, but its motive remains the same – to introduce you with yourself. It comes when you're undergoing different phases of life and find yourself doing what you thought you never would.

NOVEMBER 19

"Each today, well-lived, makes yesterday a dream of happiness and each tomorrow a vision of hope. Look, therefore, to this one day, for it and it alone is life." —Sanskrit poem

The more enthusiastically you live in the present,
the more hopeful you are for tomorrow.

It is mandatory for a person to stay wakeful to the blessings of today and live to the fullest. For this sets hope for a better tomorrow and even better future. And this comes from a keen sense of the fleeting time that we have on earth. The wise live their today to the fullest just in case there is no tomorrow.

NOVEMBER 20

"When there is love in your heart, everything outside of you also becomes lovable." — Veeresh

In order to adored, you ought to spread love.

We admire people for the vibes they get across. Hate begets hate; love begets love. What you give is what you receive. For a person who has so much love inside his heart that he couldn't do without sharing, tend to receive the same level of love, let alone respect for who they are. Society calls them charming, and charm gets most of the things done.

NOVEMBER 21

"Only in quiet waters things mirror themselves undistorted. Only in a quiet mind is adequate perception of the world." —Hans Margolius

The stirred-up cloud of mud is blinding. You
can only see when the mud settles.

O nly the quiet and calm can make the picture clearer for you for it is the serenity and peace that makes the picturesque beautiful and poetic rather than the storm, which is all chaotic and tremor-ridden.

NOVEMBER 22

"All changes, even the most longed for, have their melancholy; for what we leave behind us is a part of ourselves; we must die to one life before we can enter another." —Anatole France

In order to achieve one thing, you got to lose on another.

E very great thing comes at a price. We lose a part of ourselves for the gain of something bigger. We lose sleep to prepare for the exam tomorrow, energy and sweat to accomplish our goals and wealth to make our business work.

NOVEMBER 23

"The ache for home lives in all of us, the safe place where we can go as we are and not be questioned." —Maya Angelou

We all are homesick for a place where all the peace and serenity of senses reside.

H umans are a bit psyched up today. And what adds to the chaos and disorder is the noise of the crowd with each one imposing their opinions and setting certain norms for us to stay inside the box. Some of us are even exhausting ourselves up in practicing daily routines and doing what we aren't meant to do. This is precisely why we all need an escape from the noise of wrongs and right and reside somewhere serene.

NOVEMBER 24

"If you would be a real seeker after truth, it is necessary that at least once in your life you doubt, as far as possible, all things." —Rene Descartes

You ought to have doubts, every once in a while,
to break the rigid walls of your belief.

The real truth seekers are always out and about in the mission of seeking the realities of life. They don't abide by the belief system and always keep their minds open to all the possibilities of life. After all, there is nothing in this world that you can be sure of.

NOVEMBER 25

"Some people, no matter how old they get, never lose their beauty - they merely move it from their faces into their hearts." —Martin Buxbaum

You ought to keep your inside beautiful.

The beauty of the face is temporary. Even if your exterior is ugly, there comes a time when your interior overshadows your appeal. You ought to keep your insides beautiful and clean.

NOVEMBER 26

"The human spirit is stronger than anything that can happen to it."
—C.C. Scott

No matter how weak we feel, we still have
the strength residing in us.

In times of tribulation and hardship, the feeling of despair is natural, but all of us have a strength hidden within us only found when dug. We, as humans, ought to find ourselves too weak in front of our hardship that we don't bother to introspect the capacity we have to bear it. It is required of us to dig deep and extract the exorbitant amount of strength that we already possess to take down the tribulations of our entire lifetime. And the question again is, do we dare to look?

NOVEMBER 27

"There is no difficulty that enough LOVE will not conquer, no disease that enough LOVE will not heal, no door that enough LOVE will not open, no gulf that enough LOVE will not bridge, no wall that enough LOVE will not throw down, no sin that enough LOVE will not redeem..." —Emmet Fox

There is no disease on earth that can't be cured with love.

Most of our diseases are linked to our psychology. When a patient is sick, and he approaches a doctor who is rude, he ought to get even sicker. But if the doctor is kind and compassionate, half of his sick feeling withers away then and there. Hence, it is love that needs to be spread through words and demeanor to make the world a better place.

NOVEMBER 28

"Faith is the bird that feels the light and sings when the dawn is still dark." — Rabindranath Tagor

Faith keeps you strong during the storm and
seizes the light out of the dark.

It is required of the human to have faith in times of adversities for it is the only thing that gets them out of the dark.

NOVEMBER 29

"Love all God's creations, both the whole and every grain of sand. Love every leaf, every ray of light. Love the animals, love the plants, love each separate thing. If you love each thing, you will perceive the mystery of God in All." —Fyodor Dostoevsky

Love each of God's creation for there is mystery hidden in each.

Not a single living thing is without purpose on earth. If we look close enough at the river flowing, at the fish swimming against the current, at the special children living their life, at the birds taking flight, at the way babies are born and every way the nature operates, we'll fall in love and spend our entire lifetime praising the supreme creations of God.

NOVEMBER 30

"Love is what we were born with. Fear is what we learned here. The spiritual journey is the relinquishment, or unlearning, of fear and the acceptance of love back into our hearts." —Marianne Williamson

Wise is he who never lets the fear of norm reign over his life.

We were born with love and courage in our hearts but grew up to allow fears to rule over our lives. The real journey begins when we let go of the fears allow back the courage and love back in our lives.

DECEMBER 1

"Meditation takes place when you bring all your awareness to this moment." —Brandon Bays

> *Meditation is about waking up into the present*
> *while leaving your worries in the past.*

Meditation is always a healthy idea for anxious and past dwellers. Some of the tragedies leave their footprint in your mind and tries to trample on all your present-day activities by taking you back. Meditation keeps you together and helps you focus on the present.

DECEMBER 2

"If we fail to nourish our souls, they wither, and without soul, life ceases to have meaning…. The creative process shrivels in the absence of continual dialogue with the soul. And creativity is what makes life worth living." —Marion Woodman

> *If we don't feed our soul, it withers and vanishes in time*
> *till we are only left with brains and no inner voice.*

Just like our bodies, our souls need to be fed. When the noise of our brains drowns out the voice of our soul, then we are at a loss. For the soul is the only divine light within us that speaks the truth and wishes well for us. When the brain is often deluded by the opinions of others, the soul is the only guide. Hence, it should be fed often by righteous deeds and heard often through introspection.

DECEMBER 3

"When we seek for connection, we restore the world to wholeness. Our seemingly separate lives become meaningful as we discover how truly necessary we are to each other." —Margaret Wheatley

> *Human is the confidant of another human.*

Humans are the healers of humans. There is a dire need every human has to pour their agony, griefs, and feelings onto others. No matter how distinctive our lives may be, we are all connected and need one another in times of need.

DECEMBER 4

"Love is a promise, love is a souvenir, once given never forgotten, never let it disappear." —John Lennon

Love has a habit of leaving its footprints behind in the
sands of time, even if the beloved abandons or die.

Love itself is a storm of emotions and sentiments. A man may forget his physical pain with healing, but he can never forget what someone made them feel. And love, owing to his cascade of emotions, tends to stick in our heads forever and haunt us with a memory every once in a while.

DECEMBER 5

"If you judge people, you have no time to love them." —Mother Teresa

The judgmental can never be lovers.

There is no room for shrewd in a house built out of love. He who judges his beloved for the wrongs and right must not be in love in the first place. Love is all about acceptance. The willingness to embrace the faults of your lover and understand the differences is what the gist of love is.

DECEMBER 6

"Love is the key. If we start to express the spring of love within that is our true essence, our Truth, our spark of Divinity... and allow it to flow more... then all is revealed. Love becomes our guide in life, our connection with All, and our path back to Source." —Peter Shepherd

One must allow love to conquer our lives; it
brings about positive changes in us.

That's the thing about love; it changes the people for better. The unloved are always frustrated, whereas the loved are always kind and generous. The lovers ought to see the light during the darkness, sunshine during the rainfall, extract relief out of pain and jot the strength out of weakness in the company of their beloved. Such is the power and nature of love. One should be surrounded by it.

DECEMBER 7

"The most profound choice in life is to either accept things as they exist or to accept the responsibility for changing them." —from The Universal Traveler by Don Koberg and Jim Bagnall

There are only two ways to cope with inappropriate
things. Either to change them or to accept them.

Unlikely and unanticipated setbacks are a part of life, and everyone undergoes it. Some people struggle hard to look ugly flukes in the eye and face it like every storm that is bound to pass, whereas some condemn the sufferings and strive to change it. Both the ways are applicable, but the sensibility is in judging the situation and trying to decide which rule to choose.

DECEMBER 8

"We turn to God for help when our foundations are shaking, only to learn that it is God who is shaking them." —Charles C. West

We reach out to God when trials come, overlooking the fact that it is God who sends down these trials.

Both the joy and tribulations are given by God. It is required of us to reach out to him during both the days and plead a way out. None of the adversities sent down your way are beyond your capacity to bear. When you say a prayer during the hardship, He is most likely to instill patience and perseverance in you to cope with it. It is only healthy to reach out to him at all times.

DECEMBER 9

"If the only prayer you ever say in your entire life is thank you, it will be enough." — Meister Eckhardt

Let thank you be your catchphrase.

Gratitude is the sweetest poem that you can narrate to someone for even the tiny bit they so for you. It stems in the doer a righteous spirit and encouragement which kindles him to continue practicing the little acts of kindness. Say 'thank you' often, even to strangers and watch the world turning into a better place to live.

DECEMBER 10

"If you concentrate on finding whatever is good in every situation, you will discover that your life will suddenly be filled with gratitude, a feeling that nurtures the soul." — Rabbi Harold Kushner

Look for the little positives in every situation, and gratitude will automatically overwhelm you.

Mark of a nobleman is when he finds himself in a desert, thirsty and exhausted, looking everywhere for water and comes across a flower sprouting in the far corner, he forgets his thirst and utter words of gratitude over God's beautiful creation. Looking for positives makes you forget about your terrible situation for a while and tells you this is not the end of the world.

DECEMBER 11

"Be ready when opportunity comes.... Luck is when preparation and opportunity meet." —Roy D. Chapin Jr

Fortunate is the one to whom opportunity comes when he is ready.

Quite rare is the double blisses where a person finds something just in time when he starts looking for it. Though it doesn't happen often, regardless of this, we need to show preparedness at all times.

DECEMBER 12

"Your perception is your reality." —Matthias Dunlop

What you perceive is what you receive.

It all begins and ends with your thinking. What we assume to be the case ends up happening with us in reality. When we declare someone – who doesn't speak much, as rude, we stop talking to them. And we deliberately or not-so-deliberately start giving the negative vibes. When that person who was quiet for a reason and didn't hate you before, will start analyzing your vibes for worse and treat you the same. These self-assumptions can get even more dangerous if analyzed closely enough.

DECEMBER 13

"Light that is One though the lamps be many." —Robin Williamson

All the lights are the same; the torches may be many.

The purpose of light is to give a man sight. The fact that isn't of concern here is where the light is coming from and what the rays look like. So far as you're getting the guidance and sight, the quality and nature of the information shouldn't matter.

DECEMBER 14

"There are three kinds of people: those who let it happen, those who make it happen, and those who wonder what happened." —John Richardson

In your life, you will always come across three types of people: the go-getters, the receivers, and the dwellers.

The go-getters are likely to invest all their time and energy into achieving what they wish to achieve; the receivers who let things happen to them and don't do anything about it whereas the dwellers sit and wonder what just happened to them. What distinguishes these three kinds from each other is the energy input by each.

DECEMBER 15

"I close my eyes in order to see." —Paul Gauguin

You need to close your eyes to see clearly.

Sometimes things aren't what they appear to be. We are living in a world that deludes us with artificial pleasures and man-made things. At times, it just takes a trip down your soul via meditation to make sense of our surroundings and our situation.

DECEMBER 16

"You are as old as God and as young as the morning." –Hilda Charlton

A human is what he seeks out to be.

A human is a perfect balance of both the things, hope and despair, joy and grief, strength and weakness, tired and energetic, old and too young to carry out actions. And it is the balance of these two traits that gets us going as no single phase should stay longer than required.

DECEMBER 17

"The moment one gives close attention to anything, even a blade of grass, it becomes a mysterious, awesome, indescribably magnificent world in itself." –Henry Miller

Pay attention! For things that appear little and
inconsequential aren't in fact as little and inconsequential.

The little things we take for granted aren't as little as we assume them to be. These little moments integrate to bring drastic changes in our life. it's required of us to be watchful of the inconsequential things that make up our reality so not to weep over the consequences later.

DECEMBER 18

"Lord, make me an instrument of your peace... Where there is hatred, let me sow love; Where there is injury, pardon; Where there is doubt, faith; Where there is despair, hope; Where there is darkness, light; Where there is sadness, joy; O Divine Master, grant that I may not so much seek to be consoled as to console; To be understood as to understand; To be loved as to love. For it is in giving that we receive; It is in pardoning that we are pardoned; And it is in dying that we are born to eternal life." Prayer of St Francis

For everything in life, we have two wings, for good, there is bad,
for joy there is sorrow, for weakness, there is a strength, for
despair there is hope, and one fluke is void without the other.

God has engineered the vast universe with balance where there are all seasons – summer, winter, spring, and autumn. When the sun sets down, the night prevails, when the rain stops, sunshine scatters, and when the hope runs out, blessing arrives. Same is the nature of man, who experiences two sides of emotions and worries when his pain doesn't perish. What one needs to be aware of is that both are part of life and temporary.

DECEMBER 19

"Love is unconditional acceptance. It is love of parents for child; also the no possessive love of partners; also the caring love between all people that enables forgiveness. It's above energy, though it may be expressed energetically. It's our essential nature: Spirit itself, the quality we share with God. And it is the binding force of the Universe, inherent in all that is." —Peter Shepherd

Love is all about acceptance and forgiveness.

When you are in love, you tend to overlook the flaws of your beloved and accept her for who she is. In love, you ought to forgive more often and accept the differences, and that is what every human is required to do – be in love or not in love.

DECEMBER 20

"To err is human; to forgive, divine." —Alexander Pope

Humans tend to make mistakes, but
forgiveness is the greatest of virtue.

The sign of the strongest man is that he forgives as quickly as his anger fades away. Not everyone is capable of having this unique trait in them.

DECEMBER 21

"Love... if you don't have it, no matter what else you may have, it's not enough." —Ann Lander

Love, alone, is enough to treat all the
evils and cure all the diseases.

Love conquers all. Love is the biggest blessing of life. It can heal a person from every trauma and difficulty he goes through. Love can make you stand against all the evils of life.

DECEMBER 22

"All truly wise thoughts have been thought already thousands of times; but to make them truly ours, we must think them over again honestly, till they take root in our personal experience." —Johann von Goethe

The secret of making a thought part of our experience is to
think it thousands of time over till it becomes our action.

If you plan to start anything, don't hesitate to experiment with it. Work for it accordingly, take necessary actions to execute it and make it a reality.

DECEMBER 23

"When we feel passion for something, it is because we are remembering what it was that we came here to do. The more passion we feel, the more in alignment with Source we are, allowing this energy to pour through us with no hesitation. This is the way it was meant to be." —Karen Bishop

We often confuse our purpose with something that we are strongly fond of – be it a person, place or thing.

I t's not necessary that what we are really fond of is our purpose of life. We need to think in a broader spectrum. We often confuse our interests with our needs.

DECEMBER 24

"Go out looking for one thing, and that's all you'll ever find." — Robert Flaherty

The narrower your vision, the more conservative your approach.

I f you limit your thoughts, then you will only come across limited things. In order to have a vast experience of everything, you need to be open-minded and accept every approach.

DECEMBER 25

"True religion is the life we lead, not the creed we profess." —Louis Nizer

We reflect the teachings of our religions through virtuous actions.

W hatever we do is the reflection of how we are raised up and what our religion has taught us. Always treat others with kindness and show your best side to reflect your background.

DECEMBER 26

"Know that although in the eternal scheme of things you are small, you are also unique and irreplaceable, as are all your fellow humans everywhere in the world." — Margaret Laurence

Everything and everybody is pretty much replaceable. So, don't psyche yourself up over losses. One door closes another one opens

Never give up if you fail once miserably. There is always another opportunity waiting for you when one chapter closes. Avail it and keep going. There is a victory after a defeat.

DECEMBER 27

"Only that day dawns to which we are awake." —Henry David Thoreau

We only appreciate the dawn when upon waking up early.

In order to witness the good times of our life, we need to work hard.

DECEMBER 28

"Ask, and it will be given you. Seek, and you will find. Knock, and it will be opened for you. For everyone who asks receives; he who seeks finds; and to him who knocks, the door will be opened" World English Bible, Mathew 7.7

In order to open any door, you need to knock first.

You ought to be a doer and an action-driven person in every way. For everything you aspire to achieve, you tend to stand up and employ all your energy and will into doing that thing. When you truly want something, you need to ask for it in order to be given;

when you're seeking out something desperately – be it education or knowledge, you get it because of your drive to achieve it. It's the first attempt that you need to make, the next follows automatically.

DECEMBER 29

"Gratitude unlocks the fullness of life. It turns what we have into enough, and more. It turns denial into acceptance, chaos to order, confusion to clarity. It can turn a meal into a feast, a house into a home, a stranger into a friend. Gratitude makes sense of our past, brings peace for today, and creates a vision for tomorrow." — Melody Beattie

Gratitude works like magic if expressed. It thaws out the coldest heart, stems acceptance from denial, drives love out of hatred, brings peace and a ray of hope for tomorrow.

Gratitude has the power to spark the feeling of love and compassion in the hearts of the kind and evokes more of such generous gestures out of the doer. It encourages the person to make a little positive impact on the life of everybody he comes across through generosity and kindness.

DECEMBER 30

"Your thoughts are like the seeds you plant in your garden. Your beliefs are like the soil in which you plant these seeds." —Louise Hay

We harvest what we sowed.

Our mind is the garden and thoughts are opinions. Our opinions spring forth from the fertile soil of beliefs. The bad thoughts are weeds, whereas the good thoughts are fruits. It's often unto us to pluck the weeds every now and then and keep sowing the seeds of hope and compassion.

DECEMBER 31

"If people knew how hard I had to work to gain my mastery, it wouldn't seem wonderful at all!" —Michelangelo

*People only look up to success, not the amount
of effort employed into achieving it.*

I f people realize how much hard work has been put into becoming a success, they would stop envying the achiever and praise him for the richly deserved victory.

Printed in the United States
By Bookmasters